MAURA'S BOY

A CORK CHILDHOOD

CHRISTY KENNEALLY

MERCIER PRESS

First published in 1996 by
Mercier Press
PO Box 5, 5 French Church Street, Cork
16 Hume Street Dublin 2
Trade enquiries to CMD Distribution
55A Spruce Avenue Stillorgan Industrial
Park Blackrock County Dublin

© Christy Kenneally 1996

ISBN 1 85635 151 3

10 9 8 7 6 5 4 3 2 1

A CIP record for this title is available
from the British Library

Cover photos courtesy of the author
Cover design by Bluett
Set by Richard Parfrey
Printed in Ireland by ColourBooks,
Baldoyle Industrial Estate, Dublin 13

CONTENTS

THE AUTHOR

Christy Kenneally was born in 1948 on Cork's Northside.

He has published two books of poetry under the Gilbert Dalton imprint: *The Joseph Coat and Other Patches* and *Out Foreign and Back.*

Under the imprint of Paulist Press, USA, he has published two books of poetry for children: *Strings and Things* (Winner of the best children's book award, CPA Awards, USA) and *Miracles and Me.*

A book of reflections, entitled *Passio*, was published by Veritas in 1995.

Christy Kenneally is now the director of a communications training company, devising and implementing communications training workshops at home and abroad. He is acknowledged internationally as an expert in the area of communicating with people in crisis. In this respect, he is the author of two audio tapes: *Communicating with the Sick and the Dying* and *Sorry for your Trouble, Helping the Bereaved.*

INTRODUCTION

The stories we loved as children in Cork's northside were stories about the childhood of our elders. The fire spat, the terrier twitched and we sat entranced on any available lap. These stories were a glimpse of the past and a setting for the present. They also gave us access to the loves, laughs and tears that shaped their lives.

My mother Maura died when I was five years old.

In the vacuum that followed, the stories of our kin assured me that I belonged to a 'long-tailed' loving tribe who would protect me from the dark.

Maura's Boy deals with the first ten years of my life. It is made up of the memories I have carried from that time into adulthood. It is not a history of that decade but rather a history of the heart so the facts are always less important than the feelings.

I couldn't have written this without the love and support of my wife Linda, my son Stephen and my extended family and friends. Memories, converted into stories, can become a monument of sorts to the remembered.

This is my intention and my hope.

Christy Kenneally, 1996

1

BEGINNINGS

Cork is a sharp bark of a word. It has none of the long-vowelled music of Galway or the rapid nasal cuteness of Kerry. It hits you a clip on the ear and stands there defying you to do something about it. The old joke goes that only Cork people can be homesick at home and, like many an old joke, it homes to the heart of the truth. Many an exiled Corkman, living abroad in Dublin or Boston, has incurred the wrath of his spouse by suggesting, 'We'll go home to Cork next Summer.'

Cork is a place, a state of mind, a life-long passion for those born within the boundaries of its embrace.

My childhood city was as clearly defined as the red sandstone face of the North chapel in crisp September sunlight. At that time it was laced into a corset of hills. In later years, it would run to fat toward Blarney, blurring into suburbs on the way to Kinsale. My world was bounded by the skyline at the rim of this nest that cupped the shiny domes of Cork. Beyond that rim was Ireland, a place we studied with no great interest at school. Kerry had the highest mountain, and the longest river drained out of the flat midlands at Limerick but that big red wedge at the bottom of the map was ours. My world was smaller still, because a river bisected my city.

The Lee trickled out of the lake at Gougane Barra and moved at a donkey-trot to Cork. At the edge of the city, opposite the Mental Hospital, it fell over a weir and in the confusion of white water split in two. The narrow south channel moved self-consciously through the college, stepping down another weir to bow under the South Gate bridge. At high tide, in high summer, it loitered green and stagnant outside the labour exchange before joining its sister beyond the City Hall.

The north channel moved broad and purposeful under the Shaky bridge, flanked by the Park and the cliff of Sunday's Well. It banked left at the Mercy hospital and threw up a spume of swans on the far bank before sailing under more bridges to the opera house. Looming over its left bank, the anaemic stalagmite of Shandon poked above the humble jumble of black-slated roofs that balanced on the marble shoulders of Saint Mary's.

This was our river. It marked the boundaries between the high hills of the northside and the flat of the island at the city centre. Despite dire threats of grievous bodily harm and shouts of 'Come home here to me drowned and I'll kill ya,' we were lured, as children, down Shandon Street to the North Gate bridge. There we would climb the iron rails to marvel at the black mass of mullet or the skill of the 'strawkhaulers' as they whipped one for their supper in a frenzy of blood and small boys. Every morning, the northside workers would walk or freewheel across this bridge to shop and factory. And every evening, they would pull it up behind them like a drawbridge as they hunched into the hills for home.

The northside itself was honeycombed with neighbour-hoods. These were clustered around the main arteries of Shandon Street and Blarney Street, Gurranebraher and Gerald Griffin Street, Roman Street, Fair Hill and Blackpool.

My mother's parents, Christy and Bridget Hartnett, lived in a warren of lanes and tenements and crowded houses with half doors. This world within a world could be accessed from Gerald Griffin Street by a single arch, and so, appropriately enough, was called the 'Arch'. The Arch wasn't a place you passed through to anywhere. If you entered you belonged or you were observed until you absolved yourself by leaving. The high side was bordered by the wall of Saint Mary's Road. In the background, Saint Vincent's convent loomed behind its own wall. Christy and Bridget were part of a clan living with, around and above each other. Two of my granduncles and a grandaunt also reared families in the Arch. Years later, when my mother tugged me reluctantly to school through the Arch, we had to leave home early to give her 'talking time'.

'Is that the second fella, Maura? He's the spit of Christy Hartnett. Here's a lop for a candy apple, good boy.'

As I fidgeted behind her skirt, I was convinced that the whole world knew my Mam, and in that world, they did.

At some stage, my grandparents migrated to number four Convent Place. If you threw a stone (and I did) from the end of their lane, you could land it on the slates or on a cousin in the Arch. The Lane was off Saint Mary's Road, which ran by the sedate convent, past the unruly gate of the North Mon, on by the bishop's palace to Farna, where the country boys went to school. We basked in the boast that we had the most religious address in Ireland. My brother tried to spell it out one day for a fella in a Bronx bar. 'Convent Place, Saint Mary's Road, down from Saint Anne's Terrace, near Redemption Road.'

'Don't tell me,' interrupted the American. 'Jesus Avenue, right?'

At the main gate of the convent, a side road ran, skirting the wall to Wolfe Tone Street. Convent Place was a narrow cobbled lane, tucked into the left. On one side the houses stood cheek by jowl until they were blocked by the garden walls of the 'new houses' on Cathedral Road. Our side ended abruptly at number four. Then there was a rise of open ground which spread to a square behind the houses. This was mysteriously called the Quarry. At the high end of the Quarry was Saint Anne's Terrace. It was in a two-up-two-down house with an outside toilet, at the top of the lane, in number four Convent Place, that my grandparents came to live with their four sons and two daughters. My mother Maura was the eldest.

My parents had a mixed marriage; my father was from the southside. His street, Wycherley Terrace, had the distinction of being entered through two arches. He was the only son of Katie Barrett, who buried her husband Michael when my father was just a boy. Katie worked as a cook at the Penny Dinner to rear Dave and his three sisters. The times and circumstances being what they were, he left school early and went to work in the Hanover shoe factory. As with many of his generation, this gave him an enormous respect for education and a firm resolution that his children would have the chances he missed.

By some quirk of fortune, Dave got friendly with my mother's cousin Delia who lived in the Arch. The story goes that on his way up Shandon Street one evening, he met Maura as she came out of Ormond and Ahern's bakery carrying a bag of flour. The flour bag hit the footpath and Maura started to cry. The more romantic sources say he replaced the flour bag from his wages and Maura replaced Delia in his affections. It can't have been too serious between himself and Delia to start with as she became their bridesmaid.

Maura and Dave started a line that drew him into the home of the Hartnetts and his conversion to a northsider. She was a gregarious, impulsive girl, with a northsider's relish for ' ballhopping' (teasing) and a withering turn of phrase when she was crossed. He was shy and angular, and had a slight impediment in his speech when excited. Courting at that stage meant going for walks and going to matches. The household gods were the players in the local club and names like Jack Lynch and Jim Young could conjure thousands swathed in red and white, the blood and bandages, to Kent Station for the All-Ireland Final pilgrimage. Once Dave and Maura swayed along with the rest of them out the tunnel, waving flags at the children on the Blackpool embankment, as they rattled off to Dublin for the big game. Heady from the excitement of a great victory, he decided to splash out and brought Maura for her tea to a restaurant on O'Connell Street. Later they strolled at their ease beside the river to Heuston Station to catch the last train home. They were in time to see the last carriage leave the empty platform. 'The breath was knocked outta me,' he said, years later. 'In them days, there was no stayin' out. You had to bring the girl home.' Needless to mention, there was no phone in number four Convent Place or at any of the other numbers for that matter. In desperation, they phoned the garda barracks in Watercourse Road and explained their predicament. 'That guard was a man among men, boy. He saved our lives.' In an act of great sensitivity, often cited by my father in his honour, the guard changed out of his uniform when his shift was over and climbed the hill to Convent Place, knowing only too well that a uniform at the door would alarm my Nan and alert the neighbours. 'They'll be down on the mail train in the morning, ma'am,' he said quietly.

Maura and Dave kept their cold vigil in Heuston Station and boarded the train at half past five the following morning, 'the longest journey of our lives.' Dave should have gone straight to work but insisted on going home with Maura to see her mother. My Nan was so taken by his thoughtfulness that she forgot any lecture she'd prepared, sitting distracted by the fire all night. All was forgiven and no barriers were placed in his way when he asked to marry her.

They went to Glengarriff for their honeymoon and returned to a flat over a shop on the southside. Leaving her beloved northside was the greatest test to her marriage vows. She lasted four days. When he arrived home from work on the fifth day, she was gone. My uncle Paddy was the nervous messenger.

'Hello Dave.'

'Hello Paddy. Where is she, boy?'

'She's gone home to Convent Place, Dave. She said you're to follow her up.'

He did. Shortly after that, they got the key to number six, just two doors down from my grandparents. It was as far away as she would ever voluntarily move and that became my home.

2
—

HOME

God turned the dark into light, and so did I. 'You turned night into day,' my father said. 'We'd be walking the floor at all hours of the night trying to pacify you and then you'd be out to the world for the day. We were jaded from you. I remember coming home from work one day and your mother stopped me on the step. "He's inside asleep in the front room," she said. "I beseech you in the name of all that's good and holy, don't wake him." I swear before God, I only put me eye to the crack in the door and you were off. 'Twasn't wishin' for me.'

Well, who could blame me? I had come from the glow of paradise to this half-light, peopled with monsters who leered into my pram making loud noises.

Most of my early memories are woven of light and water and Maura, my mother. Somehow it is always summer in these recollections and I am sitting on the step outside the front door. From this high throne, close to the sanctuary and safe from harm, I could oversee the doings of the day. There was a regular and comforting rhythm to the cycle of life about us. The women woke early, usually to the crying of a child. They rattled the range awake and set the porridge burping on the stove. Then the men were called for work. One of the jokes we loved as children was about the small boy at catechism class who was asked: 'Where did the Holy Family live?'

'In Blarney Street, Miss.'

'How do you know that?'

'Well, when I was coming down to school this morning with me Mam, I heard a woman shoutin', "Jesus, Mary and Joseph, get outta dat bed."'

My father always hit the floor running, maybe because the lino was so cold or, more likely, because he hated to be late for work. In later years, he would go immediately and hammer on the bedroom wall. 'Right, Dave', Johnny Mul would answer sleepily from next door. Washing and shaving was done in the kitchen sink, his braces dangling down behind him. He said his morning prayers there as well: 'Oh sweet sufferin' God!' as he splashed cold water in his face.

Click-click-click, Bertie Barrett coasted past the door, side-pedalling to Murphy's Corner before he swung his leg over the bar, heading for the ESB. Peggy and Sheila were next, their arms wrapped around them from the cold, their faces stretched with sleep, followed by the heavy steady tread of Mr Barrett, a dark block-like man with lively eyes. All obeyed the unwritten code of quiet that respected sleeping children in the huddled houses. Mr O'Leary never kicked his motorbike to life until he reached Saint Mary's Road.

The children's breakfast was a mixture of porridge and whingin'. I remember the little eye-bubbles, winking from the top of the porridge and the way the sugar melted into dark lines before rich milk raised an island from the bottom of the bowl. This was my oasis of interest in the middle of chaos.

'Mam, where's me book?'

'What book?'

'Me reading book.'

''Tis wherever you left it. Wash behind your ears, you caffler.'

'Mam, we must bring a penny for the black babies.'

'Them nuns must think we're made of money. Go on, the other ear. I have me eye on you. Come here to me. Look up.'

She licked the corner of her apron and scrubbed the crumbs from Michael's face.

'Hold his hand and cross the road at Annie's.'

Then, at the door, a drenching of holy water from the font, and they were off, ribboned and capped, to school. I remember she'd sit sideways on the kitchen chair, her legs crossed, holding herself with her left hand, a cup of tea in the other, half awake in the sudden quiet of the kitchen. At last, the house and day were all our own.

We had a small house, a tiny kingdom of special places. The glass in our back door let in a square of sunlight on the bottom steps of the stairs. The lino there was gloriously warm, seeping up through my pyjama pants. I could close my eyes and float in a world of honey gold, smelling the rich polish from the brushes stacked in the corner and feeling the wax and wane of warmth as the light dimmed or strengthened through the panes.

A locked front door was an affront to neighbours. The

door was always 'on the push' for Auntie from next door (no relation) or Dotey Purcell from up the lane or Nan from number four.

'Maura, will you call to Billy's for me? Three chump chops and two centre loins, and ask him for a small bit of suet. The poppies in Annie's are like balls of flour. Have Mulcahy's any fresh bodice?'

In a time before fridges, shopping was a daily pilgrimage, a social occasion for the women of the parish, and a mixed blessing for their children. I was harnessed into the go-car and bumped headfirst out the door down to Annie's. There was the smell of clay from the potatoes piled in the corner and the clink of the weights as the scales balanced. The serious stuff started on Shandon Street. The fresh-meat shop was a shop of horrors. Crubeens were stacked like firewood on a plate, drisheen swam in a milky dish and a pig's head glared from the window. Billy the butcher's was just as bad. Lamb carcasses swung from hooks and dripped dark blood into the sawdust on the floor. Livers pulsed purple under glass, and the sounds were always of hacking and chopping and the awful sound of the electric saw through bone. Billy and Mike were a study of synchronous movement, swerving in and out to chop, cut, weigh. 'There, ma'am, a lovely piece of meat.' Then wrapped in white paper, trussed with twine.

'That's three and six.'

'Ye bloody robber.'

Ormond and Ahern's was a cathedral kind of shop, brown and aching with the smell of fresh bread.

'Hold that pan for me like a good boy. Eat the crust and I'll kill you.'

The moving was great but parking was a problem. Maura liked to talk and perform. She would have the shop in roars about the gasman or the milkman. Meanwhile, I was being mauled by her audience.

'Would you look at the white head on him. Hello, blondie, will you give us a birdie?'

Long noses jutted from black shawls and stubbly kisses raked my cheeks. The upside was the penny bar which always worked itself sideways in my mouth and stuck. Grinning hideously and drooling brown spit like an eejit, I was parked outside the post office or the snuff shop until the damned thing softened enough to be chewed. Many of the women heard Mass read at ten o' clock and read their neighbours until eleven, time to put the meat in the oven. The poppies went on at twelve and the table was set for the first invasion when the other two bowled in from school. From one to two was Dave's dinnertime. He ate solidly and stoically in a whirlpool of voices.

'The nun said . . . '

'A boy in my class swallowed the mala.'

'Drink up that milk; hush for the news.'

There was always solemn silence for the news. Then back to school and work for them and peace and quiet for the two of ourselves.

Nailed to the wall at the left of our front door, a porcelain angel held a scallop shell of holy water. It was always half full of dusty liquid. The dust was salt. I discovered this when Michael obligingly gave me a leg-up for a drink. The gas meter hung on the other side. 'I'm robbed from that,' she said. It was an intruder, a lodger, something she barely tolerated in the house.

Every morning, the threshold and hall would be scrub-bed and I would step across the archipelago of the previous night's *Evening Echo* to and fro. 'Don't put a foot on me clean threshold!' The open-banister'd stairs led down into the kitchen and doubled as an observation post above the action or as a perilous slide because of the kink at the bottom. Under the stairs, we had a 'caboosh', a sort of enclosed space, concealed by a small door. Here, the coats were hung and everything was flung that couldn't perch on a nail or nest in a drawer. I loved it. Maura ran for the Nan more than once before she discovered my hidey-hole. Auntie Nelly opened it one day to put in her shawl and went straight to confession after I appeared Lazaruslike from the gloom.

The caboosh smelled of must and mildew. Every hanger groaned under four coats of different sizes and textures but the gold mine was the floor. Under a topsoil of curtains and collarless shirts, lay the real nuggets: an iron, high-heeled shoes, a handbag with a challenging clasp and my father's metal last, which I found with my knee. I could sit there for hours, eyes closed, feeling around with my hands, guessing the garment from the Braille of its texture, smelling out the lair of a Russian boot or a pair of galoshes snuggled up together in the dark. Every now and again, I'd make a grand entrance to the kitchen, 'Da-raaan!' sweeping out of the caboosh dressed in Nan's funeral hat, one clip-on earring, a tripping skirt and odd football boots.

'He'll end up in the opera house.'

The front room had a closed door with stippled glass

panels. The doorknob was loose and challenging. Inside, on the left, the brown radio squatted on a bamboo stand. The table was solid and square, crosshatched underneath with beams from leg to leg. This was my boat above a lino sea, where I would sway to my own sea-sounds under a canopy of white wood and a fringed tablecloth. The window-sill was painted white and hosted a dusty geranium. Geraniums always had a fly-spray smell. For years I thought it did kill flies because there were always bluebottle bodies strewn across the white landscape. The chairs had a green leatherette top with an interesting hole in one which I mined for dry stuffing.

Above the cast-iron fireplace, a mantelpiece held vases, souvenirs, and geegaws of every shape and hue but the holy of holies was the glass case. Enshrined on three glass shelves was the 'good' ware. China teasets and elaborate teapots, slabs of icing from someone's wedding cake and a small silver horseshoe exhausted my admiration. This was the great untouchable, opened only by adults or my eldest sister, with smirking superiority, whenever we had visitors. My mother had a 'plank' there, a secret stash of cash in a yellow teapot. As years went by, school certificates, insurance policies and all the archival material of the family crowded the glass case. Even now I can remember with awful clarity the day I smashed the glass.

Michael was doing what older brothers do, annoying me. He was a practised disturber. Why we were in there or how I came to have a hurley I'll never know. I do know I missed him and hit the glass case. There was no dramatic crash and shower of splinters like in the pictures. There was the barest tinkle as a large jagged piece of glass landed on a teapot. For all its understatement, that tinkle was my death knell. We were shocked into comradeship by the disaster. Michael knew there would be no selective surgical strike, no smart bomb that would swerve around him and level me. Dave would discover and we would die.

We took off like greyhounds for number four, trying to get in first with accusation and excuse. He won.

'Auntie Noreen, he smashed the glass case.' The shock saved me. She deflated into a chair.

'Oh my God, and all the years that stood there!'

My bladder threatened to burst. 'Oh my God.' She looked through the hole as I tried to block sight of the hurley. Then she sat us down and calmly concocted a story for Dave. I was shocked and elated, shocked that a grown-up could come up with such a terrific lie and elated at how terrific a lie it really was. He might actually believe it. To her eternal credit, she stayed to face him. She waited until he was safely behind the table and into his tea. He listened, nodded and reached for the jam. We were weak with joy. We were the chosen people, God's elect. The avenging angel had passed us by to shag the Egyptians but we were saved. But I could see he didn't believe it. Thirty years later, I almost told him but something about that sacred repository of memories and the awfulness of its violation held me back.

Upstairs I never wanted to go. The shadows pooled on the landing and overflowed into the bedrooms. The bedroom was a place for shape-shifting. When the light went out, the shaky chair in the corner could suddenly grow another leg and move. I swear I saw it flicker in the corner of my eye. The wardrobe loomed, massive and menacing. Somebody told me of a bold boy who climbed into the wardrobe and it fell on him. My chest tightened at the thought of the suffocating dark, the boy swallowed up and gone. My father one time hung his coat on the wardrobe door and in the morning I lay transfixed in a cooling pool of terror.

Our fifth room was the yard. Our yard had high whitewashed walls, an outdoor toilet and a tap. There was a coal shed tucked between the toilet and the house. The wash on the walls would come off on your hands and on to your face and you could look in Bernie's pram and go 'Aaagh!'

'You lightin' caffler, and it took me hours to settle her!'

The sting of the teatowel lasted for ages but 'twas worth it. My father was obsessed with having a clean yard; this was linked, I believe, to his fear of rats. He thought a trace of dirt in the yard would lure them up the shore and into the house. The way he spoke of rats obliged us to kill them with hurley or dog at every opportunity.

'They'd bring a fit of sickness on us all.'

I remember sharing a bedroom with him once. We had an oil heater in the room which we hardly used for fear we'd smother.

During the night I could hardly sleep so I drummed my fingers on the top of the heater. Tippity tap, tippity tap.

'Christy!'

'Yes Dad?'

'D'ye hear that?'

'What?'

'That scratchin'?'

'Ah, that's only me on the heater.'

I had him in the horrors.

There were houses that weren't as clean as our yard. One of the fastest ways to his good books was to bless it with Dettol and scrub it with the yard brush. 'Doubt ya, boy, a great clean smell!'

'No r-a-t-s here,' I felt like saying, as if to comfort a child.

The outside world had two borders. The marker stones at the end of the Lane blocked my passage to the possibility of being trampled by a horde of homing children from the schools or a clip from a freewheeling bike. The other end, where the Quarry met the Lane, was the wide open prairie. Neilus was my pal. We surveyed the world and planned our day risking piles on the cold concrete step outside Barrett's. One special day, we stood at the foot of the Lane, our eyes closed, hands outstretched touching the wall, and traced the contours of the Lane all the way to number four: Cremin's gable end, dashed and prickly, a patch of smooth warm plaster marked the flue; Auntie's house next door to ours, the bubbles on her painted door you could burst with your fingers; our door and the window, reach up and spin the shutter clasp, then, Mul's and Hartnett's, Nan's window lower than the rest. Then round the wooden pole tingling with warnings of electrocution, the rising slope to the low backyard wall, and then, the Quarry.

Oh the wonders of waste ground! The grass was high and lush at our end, vivid with dandelions. Pluck them and their revenge was ire. Later, we learned to rub their milky sap on warts. Pull a sod and there were worms and small dried spiders. Sometimes, we surprised an earwig and ran. We'd heard the horror stories from the big ones.

'And d'ye know what happened: the earwig ate his way right through his head and out the other ear. On me soul.'

Butterflies were a real challenge. Catch the two wings and you have a butterfly, catch the one and you have a creepy crawly, legs all over your hand. We crouched like tiny Sumo wrestlers in the grass, thumb and forefinger extended, ready to grip them when they closed their wings and dance them to the jar.

The centre of the Quarry caught the run-off after rain into three expansive pools. Lollipop stick ships left a wake of smoky brown as they sailed from shore to shore, urged on by a bombardment of small stones. Sometimes, Neilus couldn't wait. He picked up a rocker and launched it two-handed into the water.

'Hey, watch out, boy. I'm soaked. They're me new anklets; me Mam will mombilise me.'

These were summers of sensations, lying on our backs, with a wary eye for earwigs, watching the small clouds sail across the skylight of our world. We fell in and out of being pals a hundred times a day. My father wisely observed, 'Parents should never get involved when children fight. The children are playing again in five minutes, the parents don't talk for years.'

There was something else about Neilus that I haven't mentioned up to now. Why? Because it wasn't of any consequence then, but it serves to show how children accept and adapt to difference. He had a speech defect, rectified in later life. I had no problem with it; I understood him perfectly and automatically translated for him.

In a group when we were deciding on where to play, I'd fill in the subtitles.

'He said he can't play down the front Quarry, his Mam won't let him.'

I never heard anyone from around the place mock him for it and a stranger never did it twice. There was one story of our friendship that became part of the local lore. Neilus must have been very sick because the doctor was called. I was at my tea at home, my mouth full of bread, and watching Michael's slice, when his mother arrived in the kitchen. 'Christy boy, come down and tell the doctor what ails Neilus.' I stood by his bed and translated for a man in a suit, who thanked me for my diagnosis with a tap on the head and sent me home a hero.

Teatime always came too soon. The deep bass Angelus bell of the North chapel rang a curfew to our play and we trailed reluctantly home. Now the early morning sounds rewound themselves as bikes clicked homeward past the door and heavy footsteps sounded up the evening Lane. Hot milk for bed, a frowning skin floating on the top, sweet with sugar and spiced with a shake of pepper. We climbed into pyjamas before the fire, then, 'Up them steps. G'night and God bless. Not a word now, mind ye, don't draw me up that stairs.' Head to toe or back to back in the bed butting hollows in the bolster, we carved a warm cocoon beneath the spread.

'Take your feet outa me face.'

'You're taking up all the room, move out outta that.'

'Why didn't you go before you came up?'

'Boys! What did I tell ye? G'night and God bless.'

There were definite rites of passage in our tribe.

Graduating from the cloth nappy to the potty was a major one, to be announced and demonstrated.

'Nan, look what I did! I'm a big boy now.'

The outside toilet was the honours course. The bowl was set into a shelf. The first task was to climb up backwards, the pants around the ankles. To the left and right were stubs of candles, and scraps of the *Echo* were hung beside me on a handy nail. Was there ever a newspaper that played so many roles in the lives of its readers? Dave bought it every evening for tuppence from the jolly paperboy on Flaherty's corner. The paperboy was as old as Dave but titles were hard to change. He was a reserved man, who called out the name of the paper rarely and self-consciously. Some of the others could make an opera out of it: 'Six a'clock *Echo*'.

With his elbows on the table, Dave would turn first to the death column.

'God help us, hah, poor ould Batna. God be good to him, he's going to the chapel tonight.'

There followed a long discussion of how old he was, where he had worked ('Sure he was years in Dagenham') and most importantly, was he related to us in any way. If that was the way we'd have to send an ambassador to the wake. Mutt and Jeff were firm favourites, to be read out and laughed at and, of course, the sports page was always a bone of contention. 'That fella is all the Bars. He had nothin' to say about the eight in a row we won.'

The *Echo* wrapped messages, covered books, lined cupboards, went up under wallpaper, was a bedding and a draughter for the fire, protected washed floors from muddy boots and, exhausted of all other uses, ended up in the outside toilet. Even there, at its lowest ebb, it could be twisted into a makeshift fag, sucked ablaze from the candle, then puffed into a steady glow. More than once, I reeled in from the yard, blue in the face.

'That boy is very chesty?'

'Sure his father is the same; it runs in his crowd.'

I loved to sit out there in a downpour. The rain rattled on the corrugated roof and gurgled noisily down the shore outside. Thin wooden walls gave it an air of fragility as if the merest membrane separated me from the elements. The other great thing about the outside toilet was that they would forget you were there. I always had big ears. They stuck out from the side of my head like indicators on a Ford Prefect.

'Maura, you should glue back his ears.'

'Yerra, he'll be alright when his hair grows.'

For a time I worried that because of these lugs if a big wind came I'd be blown away. One dawdly sunny morning near summer's end, they picked up the first signals of impending doom. Maura and a neighbour were chatting in the kitchen, the back door open, 'for a breath of air'. I filtered out their small talk until school was mentioned.

'Isn't he a bit young yet?'

'Sure he was four last April, girl. I have his name down in the Pres.'

'I still thinks he's a bit young. Wouldn't you hold on to him till next year?'

'No, he'd miss a book, and, anyway, he's runnin' wild around the place.'

This was serious. School was where the big ones went. According to them, you sat in a desk all day and put up your hand to go to the toilet. Why anyone would sit in a desk when they had only recently escaped from the captivity of the high chair was a mystery to me. Even more puzzling to me, from my lofty perch on the outside toilet, was why you had to put up your hand to go! The big ones also talked dramatically about slaps and something fearsome called a 'bata' which the nun kept in a special cupboard. I didn't like the sound of that animal at all. School was something we small ones played in the Quarry. We made a square of loose stones, and brought pieces of slate and a sharp stone for paper and pen. A girl always bossed her way to being the teacher. She put on an adenoidal Montenotte accent which jarred with the optional 'th-s' of our area.

'Now chuldrun, show me yur nails. Oh, look at dat: yur nails is turrible. Dis is de way to keep dem clean.'

This was not encouraging for a boy with an aversion to the facecloth. The pressure began to build as the summer waned. Nan bought my new school sack and presents of pencils and a rubber appeared. I played along to humour them, fitting on the sack that fastened in the front, and parading in my new knitted pullover, short pants and kneesocks. But I resolved in my heart that I would not go, sure she couldn't make me. The dreadful day dawned and we were tumbled to the lino, filled with porridge and swiped with a face cloth. As she took me by the hand, I lay out flat on the floor, passive resistance. Maura was made of sterner stuff.

''Tis up to yourself now. You can lie like that and be dragged to school or get up, like a good boy, and walk, but down to school you're going.'

She was true to her word; halfway out the hall I got up and surfed behind her down the hill. We wheeled left at Hill's shop, another cousin, and plunged down the Lane to the brown door. I was caught up in a stampede of new sacks, red eyes and runny noses, and she was gone.

Actually, it wasn't so bad but I wouldn't give her 'the soot of it'. She had broken the bond and now, she would pay. I usually started whingin' at Keating's on my way home from school. By the time I turned the corner into the Lane, I had changed gear twice and had a tuct in my heart. Eily Leary, an adopted aunt, was soft-hearted to a fault.

'What happened you boy? Did you get a slap? I'll go down and soften her face for her.'

I was well into my agony by the time the door opened. I wouldn't tell her anything; just rubbed my nose in misery along my sleeve. I had her distracted.

Delia lived in the Arch and Maura brought me there one evening after school.

'I'm demented from him, Delia. He has me disgraced every morning.'

Delia took me by the hand.

'Come out here boy 'til I show you something.'

Intrigued, I trailed her to the spacious back garden. Chickens! They were everywhere, picking and clucking and scratching all over the place. She bent into a box and wiped something on her apron.

'Now, Christy, if you're a good boy and go to school for your mother, you can call to my door for one of them every day,' and she put a smooth brown still-warm egg into my hands. Oh, the wiles of women, my education had begun.

We had a lady teacher who wore thick brown stockings. Every morning, after the half-nine bell had sounded from the chapel, we lined up in the yard and filed into school singing, 'Half-past nine, plenty time, hang your britches on the line.' We sat in wooden desks with a groove along the top for pens and a hole for the inkwell. Religion was big on the agenda and we started the day with the Hail Mary. Wacker sat beside me. He was a 'wilder' and I was in awe of him. 'Hail Mary,' she'd intone in a loud voice. 'Full of grace,' we roared back. 'The Lord is a tree,' Wacker whispered. God, he was desperate. I loved him. When we went to the yard for our break, we got an aluminium 'ponny' of watery milk and a dry bun. Sometimes, Wacker produced a length of twine which he looped around my neck and under my arms as reins. Then horse and driver, we galloped around the yard scattering the girls. Later in the day, we had, '*Teir a chodladh*' [go to sleep]. On that instruction, we folded our arms and laid our heads on the desks for a sleep. 'Hey Wacker?'

'Wha'?'

'What does she do while we're *a chodladh*?

'She changes her nylons!'

Neither of us slept much after that.

The Lane outside the school had a soft yellow-brick wall. We could scrape some of the dust into our palms, spit to make a mixture and polish a penny to pure gold. While we were starting the best days of our lives, the pigs in Denny's bacon factory were losing theirs and the air resounded to their squeals. The factory smell was all-pervasive to the point that the locals ceased to notice. Across the road, in Gerald Griffin Street, the vegetable shop overflowed into crates along the path. Almost every day, I took a carrot from the stall and chewed it thoughtfully all the way home. In later life I was convinced that the combination of Delia's eggs and the stolen carrots gave me high cholesterol and terrific eyesight.

The really great days were when the priest called. 'God bless the work.' Father O'Sullivan was bigger than Dave and he had wavy black hair over a red face. As soon as he walked in the door, all semblance of sanity and order flew out the window. Like all children, we recognised and responded to an adult who was a bigger child than ourselves. He drew us into occasions of sin, vying with each other to tell the tallest tale. Then he would put his fingers in his mouth and whistle long thrilling bird calls. Sometimes he got totally carried away and, to the teacher's confusion, declared a half-day. We boiled around him, tugging at his coat for notice.

'What's your name boy? Sure I know your Nan well and your uncle Josie.'

He did and would appear at home for the dues.

'No, no ma'am. I'm only up from the table. Well, if you're sure you have enough,' and he'd put his long legs under the table like the rest of us.

I found the lessons easy enough, rattling off the tables with the help of fast fingers, but reading was my passion. A houseful of comics was a great incentive but I longed to do more than look at the pictures. The real story was in the balloons that came out of their mouths. Little did I know that cracking that code of letters and gaining access to the plot would limit my imagination but it did, as television would do to a generation reared on the radio.

There was yet another ritual I had to experience before I could be classed a 'big boy', a haircut. Maura's skills as a stylist were limited to the 'bowl' cut. She simply combed it all down flat and snipped the fringe in a straight line all round. Now that I was a schoolboy, I could go on Saturday with Michael and Dave to Mr Regan's. His shop was a single room at the top of Gerald Griffin Street, beside Coleman's. It was no bigger than the front room at home but was magnified by the two large mirrors on the wall. Two enormous highbacked chairs squatted before the mirrors. These were covered with red leather and had arm rests. A plank across the arm rests was a seat for a child. Arrayed before the mirrors on a narrow shelf were all the tools of the trade. It was filled with bottles of hair oil, some of them two-toned, and cards of styptic pencils and combs. The lino always wore a soft drift of hair and a padded bench ran around the wall. But the glory of the shop was overhead. Cages of canaries, finches and linnets bordered the wall at ceiling height. We sat under their cages reading our comics waiting our turn, hoping that that small bump on the head was corn. Mr Regan was a small balding man, trim and tidy, with the erect bearing and direct clipped manner of an old soldier. The men would hang their caps behind the door and shuffle into the seat for a shave. Mr Regan swung the cloth around them like a conjuror and tucked the top inside their shirts. Then he sharpened the ivory-handled open razor on a leather strap. The ritual involved laying a hot white cloth over the face while he arranged a piece of paper on the victim's shoulder, so he could wipe the excess from the blade. The talk never faltered. Dogs, birds, matches, hunted, flew and played around the room in rapid-fire argument. Mr Regan was in the thick of it, varying the sweep of the razor to match the intensity of the debate. Speed had no place in his vocabulary nor was it expected by his patrons. As small boys, we preferred Finbarr, his son, a gentle smiling young man who was the soul of tact and good humour. When my turn came, I was hoisted on to the plank. Mr Regan pushed my head forward with his left hand and held the hand-worked clippers in his right, plying me with riddles along the lines of: 'If a man and a half dug a hole and a half for a day and a half . . . ' He was an original barber, committed to the simple concept of the haircut. You paid your shilling and that's what you got, right into the bone. 'There you are now, boy: that'll keep you going for another while.'

Head suddenly cold, I would rush home to wash my hair in the sink and soothe the prickling of small hairs inside my collar.

My worst day in school was the day I had 'a little accident'. The fact that I considered myself a 'big boy' made it all the more awful. I suppose the warning signs were evident. I was feeling frettish that morning and had a pain in my stomach, which Maura diagnosed as 'school-itis', a regular condition that cleared up by being ignored. It didn't and halfway through the morning, the inevitable happened. Wacker was subtle as ever.

'Miss, I tink he's after doin' his number two.'

I remember she kept her distance, standing in the aisle of desks near the top.

'Why didn't you put up your hand? Go on, go straight home.' It was the longest journey of my life. I hobbled up Gerald Griffin Street, trying to keep to the dry front of my pants, my disgrace trickling disconsolately into my socks. Maura was out and the house was being minded by Mary Kate, a distant relative. Mary Kate hadn't chick nor child and was ill-equipped for this emergency.

'God, you're home very early. Your Mam won't be long. What's wrong? Oh Jesus Mary and Joseph, go out in the yard quick and take off that pants.'

I stood in the middle of the yard miserable and crying, my treacherous trousers pooled around my feet, as Mary Kate connected the hose to the cold tap and sprayed me. I remember thinking then that nothing worse could ever befall me but I was wrong. Already the clouds were gathering at the edges of my world and when the lightning struck, the world I knew would be no more and I would never be the same again.

3

MAURA

The year 1953 is a shattered mirror. There is no complete picture of events in my mind, only sharp and painful slivers. I remember Maura had a headache and I had to be a good boy and hush. We were standing in the limed backyard, pale with reflected sunlight. She took a drink of water from the outside tap.

'God, I think I've swallowed a spider.'

There was a song doing the rounds at the time about an old lady who swallowed a spider that 'wriggled and wriggled and tickled inside her'. The last line was: 'Perhaps she'll die.' I watched her very carefully but she managed to make it back to the sanctuary of the kitchen, moist and warm with the smell of ironing. Our Nan began to spend more time with us than she did in number four, to give Maura 'a bit of a break'. Neighbours, who would normally breeze into the house, came cautiously, wrapped in shawls, perching on the edges of kitchen chairs.

'How is she, ma'am?'

'The same, girl.'

'We're stormin' heaven for her.'

'Sure I know that.'

One of the visitors brought grapes in a damp paper bag and distractedly handed them to me. I went up the stairs to her bedroom, my hands and jaws moving very fast, my feet moving very slowly, and sat at the end of her bed.

'Oh grapes! Are they for me?'

'No,' I replied, 'they're mine,' and ate every single one. Being good was an awful strain and the games in the Quarry were a great escape into normality.

'She's gone up to Dublin, shifted. Sure 'tis all in the hands of God now.'

Dave and my grandfather disappeared and Auntie Nelly, my Nan's sister, became a fixture. Good news percolated from the kitchen through the lattice of the bannisters to the small group huddled in pyjamas on the stairs.

'Dave and Pop are staying with the Donovans in Dublin.' Paddy, Liz and their daughter, Hannah, our Dublin cousins, opened their hearts and their home to the two men who kept the vigil at her bed in Saint Vincent's on the Green.

'Wait 'til I tell you. When Dave and Pop went home for their tea, she was sitting up in the bed. "Here's Paddy," she told the nurse, and Paddy walked into the ward all the way from America.'

These were sparks of hope to be fanned in the telling and retelling as they waited.

There is a scene that is printed indelibly in my memory. Nan and Auntie Nelly sit flanking the fire in number four. They seem to be listening for something and this quells our talk. Kay, my eldest sister, is sitting upright on the green-topped chair near Nan. She is wearing her school gymslip and sits very upright, her hands in her lap, her feet crossed. She too seems to be listening. Michael and I are sitting on the mat before the fire, giddy with uncertainty. Even Bernie, the baby, is hushed by the mood of the room. There are heavy footsteps outside the window and the front door opens. Pop, my grandfather, and my father loom large in their belted overcoats. My father's face is tight, a mask of high white cheekbones and shadows. Pop's powerful shoulders are lost in the big coat, his normally bright round face is stretched into a puzzled expression. He looks at my grandmother and shakes his head. Nan and Nelly begin to cry, a terrible suffocating soundless crying that pulls their lips inwards and their eyes closed. Kay joins their crying from the chair. Michael and I are skitting with fright while Bernie looks from one to the other, lost.

We were farmed out to relatives for the funeral. It was the way at the time. There would be scenes they thought we shouldn't witness and perhaps, our reactions would be too much for them to bear. Auntie Noreen's friend, Monica, spirited us away to a high house in Blarney Street where herself and her sisters tried to distract us with songs from the show in the opera house. At some stage, I was sent to a cousin in Spangle Hill, a woman about my mother's age who had a big girl and a boy almost as old as me. His name was Eddie. She fussed over me in a distracted kind of way. Once, she came out of the kitchen, her apron to her eyes.

'Are you cryin'?' I asked her.

'Ah no, boy,' she said quickly, 'I'm making chips.'

That made perfect sense. Chip shops were beginning to become popular on Fridays and my Dad disapproved of them. He said that chips weren't proper food at all and only lazy mothers got them for their children. She was ashamed of herself. Well she might cry! But, there was something wrong, something very wrong. I was getting too much attention and no correction. Eddie innocently added to my foreboding. Probably threatened into generosity by his mother, he produced a biscuit tin full of Dinky toys.

'You can play with them if you like.'

When five-year-olds play there is an understanding that: 'What's yours is mine and what's mine is me own.' There was something very wrong. We arrived home to find black crepe on the door. All the women looked pale and washed-out in black skirts and cardigans and my father wore a black tie and a black cloth diamond on his sleeve. I will never forget their eyes, red rimmed and haunted as if constantly on the verge of tears. None of them had an ounce of energy. Only Bernie asked the question that choked the rest of us.

'Where's me Mam?'

'She's up in Dublin in hospital love, sure you know that, out now and play.'

We were building a dam to block the narrow channel in the Lane when Bernie nudged me.

'C'mere, Mammy's dead, you know.' She said it in her matter-of-fact ould woman's voice.

'Who told you that?'

There was always some scut who delighted in telling small ones things they didn't need to know.

'Sure they're all saying she's up in Dublin, in hospital,' she continued. 'She is in me eye.'

Dead was something we knew. Early on, we had discovered a second community living in the Lane. Under the eaves of every house nested a large clan of sparrows. We called them 'spadgies'. These dusty, freckled birds mirrored the life below, chirping busily in the morning, foraging to and fro from bin to bin throughout the day in search of a crust, swapping contented small talk as the sunlight slanted in the evening and the shadows filled the Lane with silence. Every now and then, we'd find a young one dead on the Lane, a faller, all yellow beak and baldy body. We knew the rituals and went about our tasks. Someone borrowed a matchbox from Granda Sutton. He had a soft hat and enormous white whiskers. A gardener, he had never lost his country accent for all his years in the Lane. I took the good cloth from the table in the front room and this was wrapped around Neilus, as he was the biggest. Neilus held the matchbox in his two hands, out before him like an offering. Jim Mack and I were his two altar boys, holding up the corners of his cope on either side. We moved in procession up the Lane and into the Quarry, an unruly mob of mourners following behind. Then, we dug a sod and placed the matchbox in the hole stamping the sod flat again. 'Buzz, buzz, buzz,' Neilus intoned, because that's what the priest said in Latin every Sunday. But this dead was different: Maura had gone away, disappeared and not come back.

Signs of my new status were everywhere. I was bold at school one day and the teacher made a drive at me but she walloped Wacker instead. Wacker never minded a clatter on credit – he could always earn it later – but I knew it marked me out of the ordinary. Dave and Pop took us walking as always on Sunday mornings after Mass. Men would stop them on Nash's boreen to shake hands.

'I'm very sorry for your trouble.'

We came home with pockets of tanners and three-penny bits weighing on our hearts. Our consolation was the clan that spread wider and knit closer than we had ever known before. Our Nan just slept in number four, appearing at first light in our house to tackle the doings of the day. The freight of cut knees and tales from school and tears were laid in the print apron of her ample lap. I remember her as a big woman of temper and tenderness, her still black hair tied back behind her head, her hands always moist from washing and scrubbing. Auntie Nelly too became a regular, especially in the evenings. Where Nan was broad and bustling, her sister was a porcelain doll, a madonna in a black shawl. She had silky snow-white hair and milky short-sighted eyes.

'Would you thread that needle for me, alanna. That's right, lick the end of it. Are you done? Wisha God bless and spare your eyesight!'

These were the rocks who underpinned the rubble of our lives, and there were others.

Noreen and Eily, our aunts, brought life and laughter to our home. On Saturday nights, we were scrubbed in the aluminium bath and set in our pyjamas on the mat before the fire to dry our hair. Armed with forks and slices of bread, we toasted the night supper to the grate. The toast was always striped from the barred grate and flavoured with ash. My aunts would whirl around the house preparing for the 'Ark'. The Arcadia Ballroom on the Lower Road was the Mecca for northside dancers. Noreen and Eily raced around the house, half-dressed, a crown of curler thorns bubbled on their heads.

'Mam, is me hem straight?'

'You could tug it down a small bit.'

'Auntie Noreen, you have a ladder.'

'Where? Go 'way, ye ballhopper. Hold up the mirror for me.'

They made the most amazing faces streaking on the lipstick that would then be blotted on the *Echo*; where else? Their friends, the 'girls', Monica and Eileen would arrive later and the four would flounce away, leaving the front room heady with talc and perfume.

'If you can't fascinate them, intoxicate them,' Bernie would remark dryly years later. We called all the women who came and went 'Auntie', though some were cousins and some were no relation in the world. Mamie was a real aunt, my father's sister from the southside. Mamie worked in the M Laundries in the Mallow Road and came every week to 'give a hand' and collect the washing from my Nan. We knew her step and bate each other to the door because she never came empty handed. Rolos, Crunchies and threepenny bars of chocolate came with teasing slowness from the bag.

'I dunno if I've anythin' for you.'

'Ah Mamie.'

Saturday was her big day in our house. An early riser, she'd walk from the southside and announce her presence in a haze of Woodbines.

'Are ye still in bed? My God, and half the day gone.'

She had no sense of smell, and that, combined with the ever-present fag, was a lethal combination in a house that revolved around gas. Often enough, someone had to rush down the stairs to save us all from suffocation or explosion. 'Well, it got ye out of bed anyway,' she'd say philosophically. Auntie Nora Mack would also come from Grawn, and Mary Anne, who was no relation at all but treated like blood all the same. Mary Anne had a big nose. Someone remarked, to censure from my Nan, that she could 'smoke a fag in a downpour'. I was fascinated by it but was kept in check by looks from Nan. Once I couldn't contain myself: 'Mary Anne, what happened your nose?'

Nellie got a fit of coughing and Nan rolled her eyes up to Heaven but Mary Anne took it in her stride.

'A slate came off a roof in a storm, love, and broke me nose.' When she left, I was crucified for being 'pass-remarkable'. These women were the heart of the house; the fresh tender skin that grew around the hurt in our hearts.

The men, my father and grandfather, were gone to work by the time we got up, and only came into our lives in the evening. We watched for Pop at half past five and took a running jump from the low wall in Saint Mary's Road, to ride his arms to Convent Place. We hovered at his elbows as the Nan heaped the poppies, bursting out of their jackets, on his plate. 'Ye're eyes are bigger than ye're bellies,' she'd say, swaddling a spud for each of us in greaseproof paper, and we'd race off with our prize, to eat it on the road and watch for Dave. At six o'clock, he weathered the charge, striding up the path. We pecked like magpies at his tea and his attention. I remember his clothes always smelled of leather and solution, the glue they used in the factory. The creases on his palm were lined with it and we would pick it out with our nails. He had hairless white forearms and a big lump above the wrist of his right hand. 'A bullet in the war,' he said and we believed him.

On Saturday afternoons, he took us two boys to bowling matches in Togher. I hated it. I remember the deadly stop-start boredom, as men with shirtsleeves rolled up to their elbows held the twenty-eight ounce bowl in white fists and tightened up to run. They started their run with the bowl outstretched, aiming where they wanted it to go, then swung with mighty force to fire the bowl explosively away, hanging in the air to watch the flight. Another man stood in the middle of the road chanting encouragement and advice. 'Lave her down here! Toss boy!' pointing at a spot on the crown of the road, that would kick with sparks as the bowl rode the camber right around the bend. Others boiled off the ditches, flapping their coats like matadors before the charging bowl, shouting in its wake, 'All the way, all the way, a bowl of odds.'

The barrier of bridge or sharp corner would be lofted, the bowl soaring up on an intake of breath to explode on the far side in whoops and cheers. I hated it. We dangled out of him, our hands in his pockets for warmth. Eventually, he'd take pity on us and walk the bordering ditches, foraging for nests. Like many another cityman Dave had a reverence for nature.

'Stand still now!'

He would slap the ditch with the flat of his hand and

a robin shot out to chide us from afar.

'Don't lay a finger on them now lads, or she won't come back.'

The eggs were like blue marbles, in a cup of woven grass and feathers. Sometimes there was a mound of down that flowered into yellow beaks when we blew kisses. Trailing behind the bowlers, he taught that leaves had veins like us, and why the moss grew only on that flank of a tree.

In the spring, he took us under the Eight-Arched bridge to gather bluebells for the May altar in school, and sometimes, there was the bonus of a steam train overhead, hammering our ears with sound as we clung to his knees and screamed in terror and delight.

Wading happily through the purple haze, we were not to know that the lofty bridge that spanned above us, or the humbler one across the valley nearby, marked a watershed in Dave's life. Many years later, he told us how after Maura's death he would go walking, always alone, always striding long and fast as if to stay ahead of his pain. One summer evening he walked to Whitechurch to visit her grave and made his way homeward by the lower bridge. The weight of his mind was more than his legs could carry, he swung them over the parapet and sat there on a cushion of moss.

'I had terrible thoughts in me head. How would I manage? Then a woman came along. I knew her to see and saluted her. She sat up on the wall beside me, just talking about children and the way things turn out. After a while, she wished me luck and went home. And d'ye know, I was in the better of it. I got down off that bridge and went home to me own house.'

Then he paused and asked with all the openness and wonder of a child, 'I dunno was she my guardian angel?'

Murphy's Rock was at the top of the valley. We entered over a stile and passed the ruined mill to cross the stream for primroses. Murphy's Rock was the Riviera of the northside. Families left the lanes in summer to paddle or swim in the stream. The women sat on blankets, their legs tucked up under bright skirts, watching the small ones at their play. The men were in their shirts and braces, reading the paper or 'balmed out' under it. Dave's hanky doubled as a net as we swung it up under the weeds to catch the wriggling tawrneens for the jam jar. Always too soon we'd hear, 'Come on now, boys. 'Tis turning cold.' Jam jars swinging on twine loops, he urged us up the hill. One magic evening, he caught an owl. It was sitting on the sill of the mill window dazed, dazzled by the last of the light. He crept along the wall and grabbed it by the legs, then promptly turned it upside down as it pecked his fingers. After we had a good look from a safe distance, he let it go.

'Sure isn't it one of God's creatures like ourselves!'

Sundays , after Mass, we were joined by Pop for a walk.

'Put away that book and come on. 'Twill put a bit of colour in your cheeks.'

We turned at the top of the Green, passing Johnny Mahony's pub; the boundary wall of the Convent and the little house where the two sisters taught piano was to our right. Michael and I picked up the pace there in case the men got any notions. Then on by Mullane's shop and into the slope of Fair Hill past the Mon gate on our right and

Auntie Nelly's house up on a height on the left. We skirted
Leary's field across the top of Churchfield. Below us the
North chapel and Shandon were tiny and the silver thread
of the estuary wound down beyond Blackrock Castle. The
North Mon field delayed us as they commented on a
match. We saluted the Sheas, our cousins and Timmy
Delaney the bowler, then turned at the Reservoir to
downhill past the Croppy Boy and add a 'rocker' to its
mound of stones. Before us, the view ran clear to Blarney,
the blue hummocks of the mountains a faint outline in
the far distance.

'Would you look at that, Dave,' Pop would always say.
'The finest view in Ireland.'

Nash's boreen snapped with dogs of all makes and
shapes; dopey hounds with small men surfing on their
leather leads, and saucy, cocky terriers, worrying the
ditches for rats and rabbits. We turned for home again
at Mickey Sullivan's pub, a tether of dogs patient at the
door. Our two non-drinkers never broke their stride
except to let us slake our thirst and soak our shoes at
the water pump. Then, over the brow of the Hill, coasting
ever faster home for the dinner.

'I could ate the legs of the table.'

Sunday afternoons were 'down the Park,' walking, of
course, to the match. I remember the crush of the crowd
and the clicking of the turnstile, pressed up against Pop's
coat. 'Two adults please.' Our spot was behind the goal
at the city end, under the scoreboard, where Jimmy
Rourke flashed up the numbers and ran an unofficial
commentary on the game. Our Uncle Joe played for the
Glen. He shared the banded jersey with Ring and Young,

Lyons, Twomey, Mul and Creedon, the northsider's house-hold gods. Michael was infected early with the fever, swaying under his cap in perfect time with the two men to watch the flight of the ball. 'Get under it, get under it. Ah lovin' God, ref.' Sometimes the roar would soften to a hush and I'd come back from throwing stones into a trough of green water that bordered the ground. The small baldy man would stand squat above the *sliotar*, facing a massed line of blue jerseys in the goal.

'Put it over Christy! Take your point, boy.'

'Is it mad you are? Sure we're two points down. Shush!'

Alone in the sudden quiet in the eye of the hurricane he would bend. As if on cue before his baton, the bunched choirs on the hills about began a roar that mounted as he lifted, tossed and smashed the white blur into the net. The roar cracked and peaked to madness as caps flew, men danced with men and the green flag fluttered from beside the post. I saw a ship move majestically up the river behind the stand.

'Pop, look at the boat!'

'Where did we get him, Dave?'

'I don't know, Pop. I don't know.'

Home by Ford's and Dunlop's, the sidecars clattering past with cheering men and women to Blackpool; then up the hill again to Swiss roll or fairy and queen cakes, droolingly hot out of the oven. The match was replayed over the oil cloth, Dave moving the milk jug and sugar bowl into strategic positions. The excitement of a goal was too much for him so he'd stand up to tell that bit. After tea, the coats were on again for the Miraculous Medal devotions in the North chapel. We always sat on the left

48

side of the main aisle, surrounded mostly by women, as we barrelled through the hymns, Pop's bass and Dave's baritone a palpable sound all about us. 'Oh purest of creatures, sweet mudder, sweet maid,' accompanied by Herr Fleischman, the organist. The rosary droned interminably on. We perked up at Benediction as the incense clouded up around the plaster saints. Then last of all, coped in gold, the priest raised the monstrance to jangling bells, and blessed another County for the Glen.

4

UNCLES

If the women healed our hearts, and Pop and Dave propped up our broken world, our uncles, Maura's brothers, were our heroes.

Uncle Paddy was our piece of exotica, our ace card in all besting arguments. We let the others up the ante about uncles in Liverpool and London before we trumped them with Paddy. 'Anyway our uncle lives in New York and flies aeroplanes.' They were shot down in flames. Actually, Paddy was a purser with TWA. For a long time, I thought he was like a bus conductor on an aeroplane, walking up and down the aisle with a leather sack and a ticket dispenser saying, 'Fares please.' The postcards came regularly from all parts of the world to be studied for news and steamed for the stamps. Even better were the long light blue envelopes he flighted home to our Nan, crinkly with dollars. Nan would get the first read and dab her eyes as it did the round of the table. Pop would hold it a foot from his glasses, head tilted back.

'He says he's off to Egypt next week, by Jove.'

'By Jove' was a souvenir Pop brought home from

Dagenham. I tried it out a few times on the lads in the Quarry but no one took a blind bit of notice so I dropped it. We sailed up the Lane fluttering our dollars, up to our elbows in envy before changing them for seven and six in the Shandon Street post office.

'Maybe he'll be home,' Nan would say wistfully. 'Please God he won't,' we added silently, pockets heavy with silver from the States. Both houses were littered with souvenirs from his travels, a bone-handled wicked-looking letter opener in Pop's we fantasised into a dagger, and a German *Stein* in our glass case that played an unrecognisable tune when lifted from the shelf.

Nan's prayers were answered when Paddy came home. Cars were hired from O'Connors and all manner of bangers were pressed into service to convey the clan to Shannon. I was bundled into John Downey's station wagon and had a choice of laps. I woke occasionally to a soft thumping sound against the car. 'Rabbits,' said someone in the dark. 'Sure the country's crawlin' with them.' I dreamed of country roads, carpeted with furry rabbits, and two long tracks of squashed ones where our cars had passed.

He came through the gate in a shiny Yankee suit. I expected him to be in black and white like the pictures. He was smaller than I expected with jet black receding hair and a huge toothy smile. Wading from hugs to handshakes, he picked me up in his arms. 'Gee, will you look at this guy!' he said. I decided he was the genuine article. Paddy was a bundle of energy with a mad infectious laugh. The two houses crackled with life while he was home and we trailed after him like Murphy's pup.

'Can you give us a lift to the pictures?'

He had hired a car, a Zodiac, an enormous concoction of fins and chrome. 'Sure thing. Let's go!' Twelve children rushed the car. He pulled up outside the Coliseum cinema and we swaggered across the road, absolutely septic about ourselves. I remember the gawping of the queue and the embarrassment of finding we were threepence short and doing 'Eeny, meeny, miny, mo' to see who would beg the difference. Paddy never forgot a birthday and marked each one with a sensible educational present. At the time, we regarded them as just one step above a pullover or a new pair of shoes but I can remember a dictionary that served as judge and jury for years of Scrabble disputes and an encyclopaedia sent for me in 1959 that pushed the horizons of my imagination far beyond the limits of the Lane.

Trips in Paddy's humble Volkswagen to Fountainstown for a swim were a mixed blessing. Paddy and Michael loved the water and couldn't wait to be togged off and 'out of pain'. I was wary of that cold green world, contenting myself with foraging for shells and stones, watching uneasily as Paddy swam straight out through a reef of swimmers in the shallows to a frightening distance from the beach. If he drowned, how would we get home? To my relief, he'd come tiptoeing awkwardly over the stony beach and we would head for home. On the journey back, he often gave a gentle tutorial in elocution: this, that, these, and those. 'This, that, these and dem,' Michael would say to get a rise out of him but you couldn't provoke Paddy and we'd nod off on the back seat, sated with ice-cream, sleepy from the salty air. We came wide awake one day outside the City Hall when a red-haired girl slipped into the front seat. Paddy was even more animated than usual and we were unusually quiet, X-raying this interloper from the back seat. Their wedding was our first and Michael and I sang 'De Minstrel Boy' and Bernie wondered what the dinner could be like after such a huge breakfast. Mary Carroll from Gardiner's Hill was to become as dear to us as our own.

Uncle Joe was our warrior sportsman, wholehearted and passionate in his pursuit of *sliotar*, terrier or hound. Nan always said he had been her salvation when Pop was in England, supplementing her purse and table with rabbits culled from the ditches around the Brake. To a child's eye, he loomed larger than life, his frame too big for the chair he sat on, his passion too broad for the confines of small houses and concrete. Some memories are crystal-clear. We were smuggled into the dressing-room under the stand one Sunday at half time. In the halflight, we watched our heroes from behind our father's coat. Ring checked his hurley in swift nervous movements, bright and shimmering with inner intensity, locked into the private contemplation of moves and counter moves. John Lyons sat as always, solid and still, his round face wet and blotchy with sweat. Joe was hunched over, steam rising from his broad shoulders. The air was heady with the smell of oranges and wintergreen. Donie, with the bad leg, limped from one to the other, checking the band of a hurley, replacing from his store or shaking resin on an upturned palm. Now Tom Reilly appears in the middle of the room and a hush falls. He starts to speak in a low intense voice that builds to a crescendo.

'Ye have 'em; ye have 'em; ye have 'em on the run. Take the points; the goals will come.'

Like a drum he pounds the hurley on the concrete floor; then in a roar they race the steps to batter on the blue-clad foe.

Joe had a longing for fields and streams. He chased the hounds on foot or ferreted the ditches or read calm water for trout in Waterloo, with the same sure grace as he could track the flighting ball and smash it in the net for club or county to avalanche the roars around the Park. The girl who won his heart was a gentle radiant girl from the Deasys of the Commons Road, an open singing household that was Glen-mad like ourselves.

Uncle Christy inherited Pop's round face, blue eyes and softness. A mild smiling man, blessed with a wry sense of humour, he was a storyteller in the best traditions of the northside. Around the fire, Noreen and Eily would prompt him into stories of 'long 'go' and he would weave a wonderful tapestry of a world that we had never known. Characters like Klondike, the Rancher, Dinny Daly and the Bowler ranged around the room as the women gasped for air. 'Oh stop, stop!' And, in the same breath, 'What about the Roman fejollica?' Then he was off into his favourite story of a classmate in Eason's Hill school who always had his hand up first waving at the teacher to answer the question, while pulling at Christy with the other hand for the answer. Christy got tired one day of being straight man to the star. 'Now, boys,' the teacher asked, 'who condemned Jesus to death?'

'Sir! Sir!' in a loud voice, 'Hartnett, Hartnett,' in a whisper.

'A Roman fejollica.'

'Sir, a Roman fejollica.'

He was bate good-lookin' around the room. Kathleen was the perfect match, a bright and jolly girl from Kerryhall road. She was a knitter of warm Christmas pullovers and a great favourite of Nan's who loved her for the love she gave her son.

Uncle Michael was the youngest, a tall rangy man with the dark good looks of my Nan's people, the McCarthys. His visits from England are laced with memories of threepenny bits slipped to us on the sly. He delighted in our school stories and listened with endless patience as we vied to top each other. He was the one who heard our tables, admired our essays and weaned me from my inability to pronounce the letter 'r' with 'The rippling river runs over the rugged rocks.' A deeply religious man, he told me years on how his faith had crumbled under the weight of my mother's death. His own mother sent him to live in our house for a while 'to give Dave a hand'. He watched every morning as Dave swung his knees to the floor before dressing for work and last thing at night after his day, and that simple faith restored his own.

We had a fifth uncle who was really our first cousin once removed. Val was Nelly's son, an only child, and the closeness of Nelly and Nan made brothers of the boys. He was initiated into hounds, bowls and hurley at an early age and played with some distinction for the Glen. 'A great boy for the books,' the family said with pride, he got a job with the *Cork Examiner* after school. Val played a large part in our story when the polio hit Cork.

5

EVACUATION

The minor plagues of mumps and measles swept the Lane
like seasonal rain. These were expected, unwelcome
visitors and the families were geared to them. Money was
scarce and Nan was more likely to summon Mrs Geoghegan to a sick child than the doctor. Mrs Geoghegan was
referred to in the local language as a 'handsome woman'.
This meant she wasn't pretty but she had strong good
looks and a character to match them. I remember her as
a big woman with gleaming white hair swept back in a
bun. She had two lively foxy daughters at home who were
great friends with my aunts and a son Paddy, who gave
us 'spins' on the bar of his bike. Mrs Geoghegan had a
cool head for a crisis and a cool hand for a hot forehead.
We relaxed when she made an appearance at the bed,
under the spell of her slow calming voice.

'You'll have to keep him in the bed, Mrs Hartnett, and
stop him scratchin', or he'll poison himself. He'll be out
of school for a week or so. That's an awful affliction to
the poor child,' she'd say roguishly. 'Twas no affliction
at all, but I'd pretend to be disappointed to humour them.

Being sick meant being enthroned on the big bed in the back room and having the satisfaction of watching a tide of children being chivvied down the hill by their mothers to beat the half-nine bell. The mothers retraced their steps in chatting pairs, only to reappear later on their way to Shandon Street 'for the messages'. The day unreeled before the back window like a filmstrip and there was always a plastic cowboy on a plastic horse to race around the arroyos in the blankets to while away the time.

'Heigho Silver! Away!'

'Are you playin' up in that bed?'

'No, Nan, I was coughin' and barkin'.'

'Don't let me hear you again.'

'Right Nan. Aisy on there, Silver, or she'll have us landed back to school.'

Occasionally, even Mrs Geoghegan was confounded.

'You'd better send for Youngy, ma'am.'

Dr Jim Young had been a great hurler on the Cork team and with our own club, Glen Rovers, and this qualified him as a member of the extended family: 'one of our own'. A small erect man, he'd breeze in the front door and march straight up the stairs. He was kindly in a brisk sort of way, pushing the cold stethoscope up under the pyjamas, arguing non-stop about the composition of the Cork team. 'Hmm,' meant you were sick. Silence meant you were doomed. He could be merciless if he thought you were playing the old soldier.

'Get out of that bed, ye caffler, and get down to school.'

The stories about him were legion. One day, a group of corporation workers were sent to cut off the water in

Cook Street. Youngy had his surgery there on the top floor of a three-storey house. Tom, a heavy smoker, lost the toss and climbed the stairs to tell Youngy. He came out eventually with a slip of paper in his hand.

'Did'ya tell him?'

'No, boy. I couldn't get me breath at the top of the stairs and he came out and gave me a prescription.'

My father swore by him. He loved to tell the story of sending for Youngy when I had pneumonia. After the diagnosis, Dave trailed him out the hall trying to press payment on him; sometimes he'd take it and more times he wouldn't. Michael raced in the hall with a ball on a hurley. 'Put him up to bed straight away, Dave,' Youngy said, without breaking his stride. 'He has it as well.'

'And he had,' Dave would conclude in wonder.

Cuts were a different class of ailment altogether. We dreaded a fall in the Quarry and a dirty scrape on the knee. 'That'll go septic,' was the diagnosis that always prompted a good whinge because we knew what was coming. They boiled up a saucepan of water and dropped in a lump of bread. The steaming white mess was sieved off on a clean cloth and slapped on the cut. We were off, like greyhound pups on polished lino, skittering around the kitchen with the pain. 'Dat'll draw the poison,' they said with satisfaction. It gave third-degree burns as well; we'd have preferred the gangrene. Serious cuts were picked up playing hurling and were a great source of blood and excitement. Both teams escorted the wounded warrior to the casualty in the local hospital. The North Infirmary was at the bottom of Roman Street, a sprawling building with a glazed yellow-brick section that looked like an inside-out public toilet. The nuns had huge white butterfly veils and always put the plaster on the hairiest part of your leg.

'What happened him?'

'Sister, he got a puck in the poll and he was in his gores.'

The puzzled nun would throw her eyes to heaven and haul the victim inside the swinging doors. We sat importantly on the benches in the corridor, staring with genuine interest at the broken and blighted of the parish. A roar from inside meant he was 'gettin' the needle'. 'Das for lockjaw,' Jim Mack would say knowledgeably, as the whole bench rolled sideways to rub one buttock in sympathy. To pass the time, we mimed lockjaw, making terrible faces until some woman put manners on us. 'Will ye stop that in God's holy name! Ye have the heart driven crosswise in me poor child.'

At last the hero reappeared, usually in a huge unnecessary bandage, cadged from a soft-hearted nurse. 'Jay!' we chorused enviously; then helped him home by the longest possible route, basking in reflected attention.

Like all matters of adult interest, we overheard the word 'polio' from our perch on the stairs.

'A poor young fella from the southside went up the baths and came out of the water crippled.'

The southside was miles away. But this thing of winks and nods and hasty signs of the cross came closer to home. A small girl up the Lane showed symptoms and we were confined to playing Ludo on the mat before the fire. Meanwhile, the house was scrubbed with Dettol and the yard was milky white and pungent from liberal blessings with Jeyes Fluid. Somehow, Bernie escaped the blockade, wandering off on 'walkabout' like the aborigines in the comics. This fateful day she strolled past the minders up the Lane and right into the bedroom of the sick child. 'D'you think you'll live?' she asked seriously before she was plucked bodily out of the house and planted back in our kitchen. That was it, we'd have to go. Like city people everywhere in the world, the adults believed the country was the cure for all ills. The country was Auntie Nelly's house in Fair Hill, about ten minutes walk from our house, but, it was away from the Lane and out in the fresh air. This was a shock to Nelly's system. She had reared her only child in the commune of the Arch, now she was landed with the four of us, one wilder than the other.

Nelly lived in a two-storey semi-detached house up on a height off Fair Hill. A high bulging wall fronted on to the slope of the hill. A narrow path ran down the inside of the wall to a dead end and Nelly's gate was second off the path. She was houseproud without being a martyr to a mop, and the lino shone. Inside the front door, to the right of the stairs, was the front room, shadowy and full of furniture. Bigger even than our glass case and dominating the room was a massive sideboard of dark wood with mother-of-pearl inlay. Apart from state visits by Nan, this room was out of bounds for us. The back kitchen was full of sunlight and had a small porch outside the back door cluttered with picks, rakes and shovels for the garden. We followed the flight of the sun in our play, starting in the front garden in the morning and moving to the back when the shadow of the house flooded down to the front hedge in the evening. The hedge was alive with invisible birds, grumbling bees and small spiders. This was my 'plank,' my hideaway when I tired of being outrun by Michael and Kay, and wasn't tired enough to make daisy chains with Bernie. I loved to lodge in a crook of branches, daydreaming in a sway of leaves and dappled light.

The back garden shamed the bare patches and sparse grass of the Quarry. Dave came at the weekends to tease the black earth into bubble-leaved cabbage, foxy carrots, onions and rhubarb. In that fertile jungle we hunted hairy caterpillars and searched for snails, bringing them as trophies to Nelly. Her sight was so bad that we had them up to her nose before she saw them. 'Oh Jesus' she'd say, and flap us out of the house with her print apron. The hedges at the back were heavy with loganberries, bees and 'wassies' (as we called wasps), fair game for a fast jamjar. But we were after bigger and more exotic game. Up to the time of our invasion, the back garden had been a sanctuary for wild birds. Our brown spadgies were drab compared to finches, linnetts, robins and thrushes. Our spadgies were also expert at escape, streetwise to the wiles of the stalking child. The blood of generations of bird-limers bubbled in our veins. These were country birds, we thought smugly; they haven't a clue. The thrush was really provoking us, tantalising us out of the bed in the mornings with the knocking of a snail upon a stone, hopping and pecking beyond our reach. Naturally, the plan came straight from a comic. Lean a butter box on an upright stick at the top of the garden near the hedge. Tie a string to the stick and run it down the garden behind the barrow, leaving a trail of crumbs outside the box and a few crusts underneath and wait. The thrush must have read the comic too. He bobbed along the line of crumbs and right in under the box. Whip went the string, down came the box, we had him. We also had a problem. When the first mad elation wore off, the question was asked who was going to put a hand in there and catch the bird. I remembered trying to catch an injured swallow in Lyons's yard and he nearly took the top of my finger as a souvenir back to Capistrano. We were stumped. 'Dad!' Dave lifted him out gently. 'Here ye are now. Put your finger there. D'ye feel his little heart thumpin'?'

We felt ashamed that we had somehow broken the code of innocence in the back garden and promised to play boats with the butterbox in future.

Freed from the rhythms of the schoolday we hopped from the beds without persuasion in the early morning, taking our buttered bread from the table to soak our sandals in the diamond-dripping grass. The only forays beyond the gate were to Mass on Sundays or to Mullane's for the messages. It was a special thrill to pass the gate of North Mon school and look in through the latticed bars at the buildings and playgrounds empty and aching for the sound of children's voices. Nan came every Saturday night, laden with sweets and fruit; it was better than being in hospital. Nelly had a real bath and the two women scrubbed us spotless for Mass.

'Wash behind your ears. You could grow potatoes there!'

Around the fire, we regaled Nan with the adventures of the week.

'Are they driving you demented, Nelly?'

'Yerra no, girl! Sure they're no trouble.'

'Keep an eye on that caffler or he'll break your heart.'

We didn't break Nelly's heart but we broke her pledge.

'I have Yanks comin' today,' she told us one morning. 'So let ye be good, for the love of God!' She divided the dusting, polishing and sweeping jobs between us. 'And be sure to sweep under the beds.' What kind of people were Yanks, I wondered, that they went upstairs and looked under the beds? Our chores led us to explore the wardrobe in Nelly's room and we rescued a hat and topcoat that had belonged to her late husband. Michael climbed in to the hat and coat and Kay rigged herself in a hat and coat of Nelly's. They snuck out the front door and stood on the step. I ran around the back. 'Auntie Nelly, Auntie Nelly, the Yanks are here.'

In a panic, she whipped off her apron and opened the front door.

'How'ya doin' Auntie Nelly?' Michael said in a bad imitation of Uncle Paddy's twang. It was too much for her. She slumped on the last step of the stairs and started to cry. Silently we trailed her into the kitchen where she took a bottle from the back of the press and splashed a generous measure into a cup.

'I'm distracted from ye,' she said, and emptied the cup. 'And now I'm after breakin' me pledge,' she said and burst into fresh tears.

She could also be a thunderin' rogue when the notion took her. 'I must get that chimney cleaned,' she declared one evening as we toasted ourselves and bread to the fire. This statement was in answer to a down draught that nearly smothered the lot of us. We perked up straight away; this meant that John would be arriving from the Arch with his bike and brushes, the two white eyes staring out of his back face like Al Jolson in a perpetual state of amazement. Nelly had other plans and we were to be her accomplices.

'Kathleen, shove the *Echo* up the chimney like a good girl.'

Our mouths fell open.

'Will ye do what I tell ye! Roll it up in a ball and shove it up a good bit. That's the girl. Light it now with a match and mind your fingers.'

With a mixture of delight and dread we lit the paper. Whoosh! 'Auntie Nelly, the chimney is blazin',' we shouted. 'Go in next door and call Mr Barrett,' she said calmly. Mr Barrett went down on his hands and knees on the mat and craned his head sideways as smouldering balls of soot bombed all around him in the grate.

'Tis like a paper stuck up there, ma'am.'

'Well, sweet heart of Jesus protect us,' Nelly said piously, 'but you couldn't watch children.' Poor Mr Barrett covered himself in soot as he lugged bucketfuls of the black avalanche out of the grate. After she had ushered him out the door dizzy with the blessings she showered on him, she turned to face our accusing eyes. 'Yerra, 'tis the least he might do,' she said in her defence, 'and me a poor widda.'

Bedtime was a series of pilgrimages up and down the stairs for 'a bate of bread' or 'a drop of milk.' No sooner would one be settled than another would be up and about. 'I'll tell yer father,' was the ultimate threat that glued us to the beds. The old house would settle into quiet, creaking its floorboards for comfort, the heavy dark furniture soaking up the last of the firelight and then Val would come home. He'd bound up the stairs and throw himself into the bed on top of us. 'Tell us a story.' To this day, I have never met a man who could weave word-spells like Val. He had us laughing and crying as a parade of fantastic figures played out their adventures between the two beds. We threw the eiderdown over our heads at the scary bits and screamed in advance to soften the shock. 'Val, Val, come down outa that; they'll wet the beds.'

'All right, mother.'

'Ah, one more, Val.'

'Tomorrow night I'll tell ye about the witch that grabbed Joe Twomey in Shandon Street.'

Her son safely home, Nelly went through the close of day rituals.

'Say yer prayers now and remember yer poor mother.' Sometimes she led us through the rosary, the northside lullaby, the repetition of well-worn words losing us one by one to sleep until she faced into the 'Hail, Holy Queen' on her own. If it was a stormy night she would add a ballast of trimmings to her prayers. 'For sailors abroad on the sea this night, Hail Mary . . . ' I wondered what sailors our saintly grand-aunt was so concerned about. Before she climbed the stairs she pushed in every trailing plug in the house, in the firm belief that if she didn't electricity would leak out of the sockets during the night and kill all of us in our beds. Last of all, she toured the bedrooms with a Lucozade bottle full of holy water, splashing it shortsightedly in all directions.

'Did ye get it?'

'We did,' we chorused, dry and unblessed under the blankets.

'Goodnight and God bless ye.'

'Goodnight, Auntie Nelly.'

6

ALLEY UP OU' DAT

The story goes that the Sunbeam workers poured out of the factory gates one summer and headed off in singing buses for the vast green silences of Gougane Barra. As they stepped from the bus one asked another suspiciously, 'What's the funny smell?'

'Yerra, that's the fresh air, girl,' was the reply.

The wide-open spaces of Nelly's garden eventually made us headachy and fretful for home. We grew lonesome for the sunny patch of wall and the small houses leaning like shawled women whispering secrets. We longed for the smells from open doors, the sounds of familiar footsteps, the kingdom of women whose consorts came home in the evening to spread the *Echo* on the oilcloth. We were eager for the pals and hungry for the games.

It was a time before television when a free imagination could whirl a full three hundred and sixty degrees. I can't remember being bored. If the day dawned bright, the Place was humming with possibilities. If we were washed indoors, then a paper ball, tied with twine, was the only prop we needed to stage an epic contest complete with commentary in the front hall.

'Is that someone at the front door?'

'No Nan, I scored a goal.'

When that palled, I could kneel on the upstairs sill, under the shelter of the angled window and watch the to-and-fro of neighbours in the Lane. Young women and girls always wrapped their arms around themselves as they skittered from door to door. Most people hunkered down in heavy coats or scowled from under flat dripping caps. Only Dave strode easy and upright as if content in the knowledge that the rain was wet as God intended and the pleasure of a dry towel waited just beyond the door. Now and then there was a pause in the spatter of steps and the whine of complaining bikes and in that lull I felt every muscle relax and, out of focus, flowed with the rain down the grey-black slates to drop the down pipe to the gurgling Lane.

Picky (hopscotch) and skipping were girls' games we were literally roped into by bossy young wans we daren't refuse. We grudgingly turned the rope as Marie Sullivan hopped in the middle but balked at joining her chant.

Who's dat comin' down de street?
Tom McCarthy, isn't he sweet?
He's been married twice before
But now he's knockin' at Kenneallys' door.
Bernie, will you marry me?
Yes, my love, at half past three.
Half past three is much too late,
So marry me in the mornin' at half past eight.

Bernie blushed happily and Tom jerked the rope to catch Marie's ankle. Even worse was to be shanghaied into playing house. You were either the baby or the father. If you were the baby you got to lie flat out like an eejit while the young wans oohed and aahed at you. 'Isn't he very big all de same?' If you were the father, you drank imaginary tea out of tiny plastic cups, read an imaginary *Echo* and got to say things like: 'Ask your mother.'

Glassy alleys, or marbles, was a real game. You 'alleyed up' against one wall of the Lane while your opponent crouched with his backside against the other wall. His job was to hit your marble with a throw. If he missed, you got to throw at his wherever it came to rest. The rules were simple and timeless but the 'gaitch' or style was everything. I favoured the slow pendulum swing between splayed legs; others held it on the thumbnail above a closed fist and fired with ferocious power. The most important thing was to have a face on you as if you were trying to go to the toilet and couldn't. Neilus and I got tired of winning from and losing to each other, so we hatched a sting. I was smaller and slighter than him but a better actor so I made the approach to the mark.

'D'ye want a game of glassy alleys?'

'All right. Heads or harps?'

'No, you can alley-up if you like.'

I was a pushover. I lined up my first few shots where he'd have to be spur to miss them and then Neilus would happen along. 'Can I fall in?'

'I don't mind,' I'd say magnanimously and yer man couldn't be a louser in the face of such generosity. The hook was in. Now I laid them up for Neilus and he wiped the two of us off the Lane. When the sucker was cleaned out or suddenly remembered a message for his Mam, we went back to my house and stashed our hoard in a sugar bag under the bed. We were into our fourth bag when Neilus made his first confession, got a conscience and ended a great partnership.

Runaway knock was a beginner's game for aspiring cafflers. The theory was simple enough. We ran from one end of the Lane to the other, knocking on all the doors along the way. The real challenge lay in doing it twice, because the second time you were expected and could be helped on your way with a clatter or the flick of a tea towel. Influenced by Dennis the Menace in the comics, I devised a new strategy. We tied a string from Mack's knocker to Brennan's on the other side and knocked on both. The tug o' war was glorious. Thunder up the alley was another notch up the daring scale. It had to be played midweek so that the pious promises of the previous Saturday's confession would have worn off and there was still ample time to work on a firm purpose of amendment for the following Saturday. We stuffed the chute (down pipe) with papers and applied the match. A roaring whoosh went up the down pipe erupting into sparks and flying fiery papers at the roof. It was worth the three Hail Marys as we hid behind Pop's wall and listened to the language.

This was Jimmy Mul's favourite game. Jimmy lived next door to us for a time and it was fire that brought us together. Shortly after the Muls moved in, their chimney caught fire, without urging from the *Echo*. The bells of the fire brigade brought us to the bedroom windows to watch the excitement. The Lane was a confusion of helmets and hoses. The women huddled in an assortment of dressing-gowns and curlers, blessing themselves with fright while the men ran around importantly in their braces, getting in the firemen's way.

'Boys, mind Jimmy now for a while and be good,' Dave said ushering a boy into our bedroom. Jimmy had a physique that Pop would have described as 'two bits of thread and a knot'. He was a pyjamas with feet, topped off with a white luminous face and a mop of hair that frustrated combs. His most memorable feature was a pair of dark dancing eyes. The minute we saw him we went mad. When Dave returned to collect him, the bedroom was a blizzard of feathers from an epic pillow fight and we were welded to the gawky boy who was game for anything.

All the boys around the place had a fascination with fire and getting our hands on a box of matches was the Holy Grail. Jimmy was very gullible so we primed him to the task.

'Go into Bridgie's shop and get a box on your mother's bill.' Jimmy was gullible but not stupid.

'Me Mam will have a canary.'

'Den she'll have two bloody birds,' Tom Mack said sourly. 'Course, if you're affrightened?' Jimmy's reluctance crumbled. The Quarry was rich in combustibles; papers and scraps of lino were everywhere. We set up our fire and smoked papers in its companionable glow, artfully building a pyramid of bubbling lino to hold the night and the imminent call to bed at bay.

Rainy days rarely drove us indoors. We huddled under

a tarpaulin tent in the Quarry, deaf to the calls from home to 'come in outta dat,' absolving ourselves from disobedience with the thought that they didn't really want us 'draggin' dirt and filth over me clean threshold'. When a decent-sized stream coursed the centre of the Lane, we raced sleek lollipop sloops and squat matchboxes, shouting encouragement as they swirled or stuck or surfed the tributaries from the gasping down pipes. The high point of my dam building/bursting career happened in the front Quarry off Saint Mary's Road. It was the day I drenched the shawlies.

The North Chapel was the hub at the centre of five spoke roads. From their perch at the corner of Saint Mary's Road, the group of black-shawled women could watch the world go by. Whenever I passed on the way home with a message from Shandon Street, I left a bob of heads and a lapping of whispers in my wake.

'Who's dat now?'

'He's poor Maura Hartnett's boy; sure you'd know him outta dem. Isn't he de head off Christy Hartnett?'

'He is, girl.'

There were two brown puddles on a flat patch uphill of the shawlies and Neilus and I were armed with two hurleys. Our first plan was to splatter any children who passed on the pavement but they divined our intention from afar and crossed to the other side at Dineen's, well out of our range. We decided to cut a channel from the upper to the lower puddle and coaxed the water with the hurleys. I don't know what possessed me; there was something about the black shawls, sharp eyes and fidgety heads that reminded me of crows. Now crows, unlike our

own spadgies, lived in the Convent trees and could be
shelled with impunity. They were not part of the tribe.
Carefully we carved a track to a point above the steps
where we built a dam of sods. Then we swept the lake
with the hurleys, our stomachs tight and tingling with
suppressed excitement as the water level rose behind the
dam. One swift flick of a hurley and the torrent began to
move. Everything seemed to happen in slow motion: the
heads stopped bobbing and a surprised voice said,
'Madge, Madge, I'm soakin'.' Then the screeching nearly
made us wet ourselves. 'Oh Jesus, I'm drownded, ye
lightin' caffler.' The shawled sisterhood flapped in
confusion, standing on each other to escape the flood. We
raced for the sanctuary of the Lane, delirious with
laughter, trying to run and breathe at the same time, our
heads tucked down against a volley of threats and curses.
'Ye saucy scut, I'll go up to your Nan.' But, I knew they
wouldn't. Nan could be a formidable figure in the face of
complaint and had little time for that particular coven of
connyshures.

7

DE PICTURES AND OTHER DREAMS

The first picture I ever saw was *The King and I*. It was on in the Savoy and Kay minded me in to the front seats where I sat dazzled and deafened for two horrible hours. When she got me to the bus-stop, she asked in a grown-up voice, 'Did'ya enjoy the picture?' This was for the benefit of the queue. I threw up over her patent leather shoes. There were nine picture houses in Cork. The Assembly Rooms was the haunt of what the grown-ups called 'a rough element'. We slummed it one Saturday to check it out and, sure enough, the film was subtitled by shouts from the gallery. 'He's behind ye, ye flippin' gowl,' was the advice to the hero and, 'Get 'em off ya!' was the admonition to the heroine. The constant swaying sea-scapes of a pirate film were too much for one patron's bladder and with an expression of beatific relief he let fly from the balcony. Never again. The Lido in Blackpool, a local wag said, was Lourdes: you went in crippled, you came out walkin'. That left seven to choose from, which meant seven different preferences and heated arguments every Saturday. It also meant one picture for each glorious day of the Christmas holidays when our pockets were flush. On Saturday mornings, we rendered unto God by going to confession and rendered unto Caesar by doing Nelly's messages for a bob. Then the debate started.

'Yerra dat one's a cod boy; dere's no shootin'!' That was out. 'Me sister said de wan in de Palace is massive.' Definitely out. 'In de Lee, yer wan gets shot at de start.' Definitely our kind of picture. Our idea of the perfect picture was where 'de wan' got killed in the first five minutes and 'de boy' avenged her with murder and mayhem for the rest of it. We pooled our money and headed for town. Before us lay the challenge of the queue. It wasn't easy for fourteen boys to jump a line that snaked all the way to Tyler's but Jimmy McAuliffe was a natural. He was slight and freckled with a drawly voice. He also smoked which made him seem older and gave second thoughts to would-be attackers. Jimmy joined the back of the queue listing from the fourteen shillings in his pocket and wheedled his way upward as the rest of us invaded the foyer pretending interest in the shop. The shilling seats were always up front where you'd be guz-eyed after five minutes. In the roar that greeted the dimming lights, our entire row descended to the floor only to reappear shortly afterwards in the good seats at the back. John Barrett nearly got us all thrown out one Saturday. If it was raining, his mother always insisted he wore a second pants, and as we settled nonchalantly into the back row, John dutifully stood up to take them off. There was an eruption of cheers and whistles and flashing torches as we pretended not to know him. 'Sit down, ye gom! I hope you get pneumonia.'

Undaunted, we shouted all the words of the ads, giving a special yowl for the nylons ad that promised, 'The magic of Mystic is yours for the asking.' Just after the ads, the spotlights picked out the two mortified girls serving ice-cream and ice lols, vying with each other for the scarlet blush award. More whistles from the fans. Then a roar went up as Fred Bridgman ascended from the pit astride a massive organ to lead us through a medley of tunes. We were itching for action and only mildly satisfied by a selection of trailers. At last, the picture. Oh the groans when 'de boy's' gun clicked on an empty chamber! Oh the screams when a feather poked over a boulder! Oh the mad hubbub of talk when the kissing started! And the roars of relief when the cavalry charged over the hill to the rescue. All the way home, we tried to walk like the hero, our coats half-open for a quick draw, our eyes in slits, making innocent people nervous at the bus-stops. As soon as we could, we replayed the picture in the Quarry. Everyone had at least one gun and hurleys doubled as rifles. The small ones were allowed a part if they agreed to die early on and soon the Quarry was littered with small dead bodies in dramatic poses, the Lane treacherous with creeping Indians, and the villain taking twenty bullets to die. 'I'm only wounded, boy.' Jaded from our efforts, we lit a 'bona' and reviewed the trailers for the coming week, trying to sustain the magic by placing a can on the fire and getting an unselfconscious Indian to slash into it for authenticity.

I played for Cork in the 1956 All-Ireland Hurling Final and scored two goals. The second one was disallowed because it took a deflection off a jamjar. I argued the point but the referee, Mr Ryan, was adamant. 'Anyway,' he pointed out, 'it travelled over the sleeve of the goal post.' This fantasy was made possible by Mr Ryan, a bus driver from the Terrace. Up to then our games were haphazard affairs with everyone chasing the ball all over the Quarry. Everyone except me, I was as far from the possibility of injury as I could get, coursing and lifting an imaginary *sliotar* into my hand as my own radio commentary struggled to keep up. 'He's on the forty, he swings, he strikes and the ball is in the net.' Mr Ryan tamed us into recognisable teams and prefaced our All-Ireland by having us clear the Quarry of stones. We threw them in a pile against the concrete wall and that cairn survived to his memory until the Quarry was levelled and buried in smooth tar. Someone put sticks along the sidelines with scraps of paper for flags and we marched behind a band of small ones playing imaginary instruments. The team which lost the toss had to be Tipperary and the next question for the Cork team was who would be Ringy. Jimmy McAuliffe won that honour with the irrefutable argument: 'I'm de only one wit a cap.' Michael was Uncle Joe and I alternated between Joe Twomey and Johnnie Clifford. Mr Ryan doubled as the Archbishop of Cashel and threw in the ball. It was here on a patch of mud that Michael and Patsy Harte served their time in short pants to the red jersey before they wore it with pride for their county. Even Neilus and myself were to have our brief moment of glory when we played as fullback and goalkeeper for the Cork under-fifteen team. But nothing ever matched that day of pure excitement as we scourged a final goal between two coats under the watchful eye of a bus driver.

As children, the world of fantasy, the world of the unconscious was where we spent our true energies. It was not different from the ordinary world, just deeper, and we moved in and out of it without noticing the boundaries. It was only as we grew older and self-conscious that we lost that grace and divided our world into the real and the imagined. Only Seamus stayed loyal to the vision, and I think in some part of our 'big boy' selves, we envied this permanent child. Because we grew up together, his difference was unquestioned, something we adapted to long before labels like Down's Syndrome could mark him apart from us. He hit me with an Indian club one day outside Geoghegan's. I was chalking a picky on the path and must have glared when he shifted into my light to inspect the work. Without malice or anger he picked up the stick and hit me.

Nan's lap was a safe sanctuary for all ills and a repository for complaints. 'Seamus is the way God made him, boy. He couldn't help doing that no more than a baby. You're a big boy now; you'll have to learn to allow for him.'

Allowing for Seamus meant including him in all the matches. Sometimes we took on a team from Wolfe Tone Street or Redemption Road and it always amazed our opponents when we called a halt to the play so Seamus could get a puck of the ball. It wasn't all chivalry; Seamus usually owned the ball and he was quite capable of taking it home if he wasn't involved.

I remember two very special days in his life and ours. We were at our dinner one Saturday when the front door opened and Seamus wandered in. There was nothing remarkable in that; he was very fond of our Michael and would often take his chances at the table with the rest of us. But, this day was special because Seamus had made his confirmation. He had the biggest rosette and medal I ever saw. Pop said you wouldn't get it in the war. I remember that he was very upright and steady and sat down with great majesty and I remember my Nan by the gas stove, fumbling in her purse with one hand for hansel and wiping her apron to her eyes with the other.

The other day that stays with me is the day he rode the bike. For weeks we saw Mr Ryan walk up and down the Terrace holding with his hand to the saddle. 'Aisy now, Seamie boy. Don't be lookin' at the front wheel; keep your two eyes out ahead of you on the road, good man.' And then, he was side-pedalling and swinging his leg over the bar and one glorious day he rode to Blarney with his dad. His homecoming was a triumph, with neighbours gathered in the Quarry and at the windows to see him glide confidently up the Terrace to the door, his cheeks ablaze from the wind and cheers.

8

'OUTLONG'

A young fella from our place started a school essay one day with the immortal line, 'One day me and two other dogs went out huntin'.'

Dogs were part of the extended family and we had a succession of Spots, all named for Spot Hartnett, a legendary ratter who lived to be fourteen. Beaver was an exception in name and nature. Auntie Noreen had Pop plagued for a beaver fur coat. 'If that's what you want girl, that's what you'll get,' he said with a twinkle from behind his pipe and he was as good as his word. He hove home one evening with a suspicious bulge under his coat. 'There's your Beaver now,' he said, and spilled a pup onto the lino. We rolled ecstatically on the floor and tickled his little bare belly until a little fountain of pure delight rose into the air. 'Ah lovin' God. Where's the *Echo*, quick. Put that dog out in the yard.' Now a dog called Spot belonged in the yard but Beaver was born for better things. We smuggled him up into the beds or in under the glass case in the front room. One day he fell asleep in the caboose under the stairs and his scratching set

Dave's nerves jangling. 'Rats, d'ye hear 'em. Dere's bloody rats in de house.' We made a complete fool of the dog, protecting him from anything that would make him streetwise. Small wonder then he wandered under the wheels of a car one day in Blackpool and had to be drowned in the stream behind the Glen Club. We washed Blackpool with our tears and were only consoled when another sawn off mongrel arrived in the door to us.

The three dogs in our Lane were called Tiny Leary, Patch Purcell and Spot Hartnett. Of the three only Spot would have known what to do with a rat. Tiny was well-named. He was a small ratty sample of a dog who rarely ventured beyond the handkerchief of concrete outside Leary's door. Tom Mack and I sat outside his range one day sizing him up.

'D'ye know he have one glassy eye?'

'Go way ou' da.'

'On me soul. A cat scrawled out de udder wan – me Mam told me.'

There was no contesting that authority; I was hardly going to ask Mrs Mack to put out her tongue so I could check the truth of it.

'Which wan?'

'Ha?'

'Which wan is de glassy wan?'

There was a long pause.

'He'd take the bloody hand off ya,' Tom said with finality and Tiny's glass eye, like religion, became a mystery.

Patch on the other hand had two good eyes, which always seemed to be closed. He had a fat sausage body barely supported by four short legs each of which seemed to have a mind of its own. For most of the day he lay dead outside Purcell's door only shifting himself to follow the sunlight. But Patch was part crocodile: he could lie like a log for days and then pin a new postman to the wall in a blur of black and white. Spot was a mongrel terrier with all the rough tongue and twitches of the breed. Pop had him half-trained when a rat caught him by the lip and damaged his confidence but he was a mastiff in comparison to the other two.

On Saturday mornings in high summer, we whistled the other huntsmen out of bed and gathered every ould God-help-us dog available to hunt the Brake. The Brake was a stretch of hilly land below Nash's boreen, littered with boulders dropped long ago by some tired glacier. The whole place was hip-deep in buttery furze, perfect cover, we believed, for rats and rabbits. We stopped at Riordan's to cut sticks from the lilac tree then faced into the hill, keeping our motley pack in order with hup hup as if we were driving cattle. Along the route there were many stops for ritual fights, and tempting ESB poles and gardens offering relief. Finally we were whacking the furze and whipping the dogs into a lather of excitement. We never ever saw a single rabbit but there was enough shouting and barking and false scents to bring us shambling home, our dogs too tired to be fractious, their swinging tongues dusting the road before them.

Summer was full of hunting and swimming and endless light evenings for games of Release organised by the big ones. Nobody ever got sick in the summer. The small houses opened all windows, the front door and back, to catch any breath of air available. We gradually went from tomato red to dirty brown. 'Wash your knees.'

'Yerra dat's me tan, Nan.'

It was the season for old neighbours sitting out before their doors, when Pop banned the electric light until the house was thick with shadows, savouring the last red flicker over Ryan's chimney, hoarding it against the long winter. We had reason to huddle close against the winter, to keep our fire roaring in defiance up the chimney. But death did not come this time in frost-bound days. It came when new grass peeped above the March mud in the Quarry and the long fast days of Lent sharpened our appetites for Easter eggs. When the bare trees of the convent were regaining their modesty and children ventured out again on legs as white as grass stalks covered by a stone, Nan died.

Some time earlier in the year she had had a stroke. We were gathered one day on the landing so that she could see us from the bed. One side of her face was tight but she smiled on the other side and lifted her hand. The nuns came from the Assumption Convent to look after her and we were told to pray very hard. Maura's memorial card was full of prayers over four small silvery pages with extra ones crowded into the margins. Every prayer promised an indulgence to shorten Maura's stay in purgatory. Sometimes I had the mad notion that she was wandering around purgatory handing them out to the people we prayed for in the trimmings of the rosary, those 'who had no one to pray for them'. 'Here you are girl. That young fella has his knees worn away prayin' for me. Go on girl, sure I have the givin' away of them.' So we prayed and struggled quietly out of our beds every morning to the half-seven Mass. I remember kneeling in the half-empty church looking up at the golden doors of the tabernacle, asking silently would it be all right if we could keep our Nan.

'Maybe ye'd like to go out to Deasy's for a few days,' they said. It had echoes of before but we said nothing, just went to the Common's Road where they made much of us and Jackie Daly, one of our hurling heroes, came every day after work to build timber blocks with us on the floor.

'Any change, Josie?'

'No Jackie, still the same.'

Joe took us walking with his own small boy to Fitz's boreen and we took turns on his tricycle. It was on the small bridge that he told us. Michael burst into tears and I wanted to but couldn't. The dark at the top of the stairs had broken free again and filled our little house. Our refuge from night terrors and sharp memories was gone.

9

CHRISTMAS

They did their best to make Christmas for us that year. We were assured that Santy would still come and Noreen and Eily stood on chairs in their black skirts and cardigans to hang the decorations. This year, it was Pop who held the match with Bernie, our youngest, to light the red candle that would sit in the window in case the Holy Family came to call. I wasn't a bit surprised when they didn't come. Sure how could they face us?

As soon as September faded in, we covered our new and hand-me-down schoolbooks with brown paper and resurrected our sacks from underneath the stairs. Christmas was coming. October winds swept the Convent leaves into crisp kicking piles. We forswore sweets for the Holy Souls during the month of November now that we had two to release from Purgatory and finally December grudgingly arrived. At this stage we were jaded with waiting and the adults were addled from 'How many more days now?' As we ticked off the days, the rituals clicked into place. Letters for Santy were drafted and redrafted and then updraughted from the fireplace to sail in soft cinders all the way to the North Pole. It seemed to me that everything they could find in the house went into the pudding. We were allowed to squidge our fingers in the chocolate-coloured, raisin-freckled mess, before it was boiled and hung in a pillow slip from the nail by the gas stove. Michael and I took it in turns to sniff loudly like the boxers we saw in the City Hall and punch the pudding. Sniff, jab, a left, a right to the body, sniff. 'Would ye blow yeer noses and leave that puddin' alone.' Joe Louis retires to the neutral corner.

The crib was Dave's pride and joy. It was a brown hardboard structure kept on the top of the tallboy upstairs. Coming nearer to Christmas he organised trips 'outlong' to gather moss so that we could clad the walls and roof and carpet the floor. The figures were swaddled in pieces of the *Echo* and were disinterred like dusty mummies from the biscuit tin. Only the Holy Family had set places, an elastic band keeping the baby Jesus from wandering off. I thought he lay there with his hands outstretched in indignation. The angels and other hangers-on had a wandering brief and sometimes perched danger-ously in the branches of the Christmas tree. Saint Joseph went missing one year and was discovered leaning casu-ally against the rear wall admiring his reflection in a silvery tinsel ball. 'Out for a fag,' Michael said wickedly and got a clip for his sacrilege. There was a woman with a water jar on her head and she was moved a lot, probably to ease her burden. Another fella lay with his head on a pillow sleeping through the entire season every year. Dave bought the tree in the Coal Quay and made a big fuss of hanging the lights so that a red one shone through a hole in the roof of the crib. Some nights as we lay around the tree, there were mysterious toings and froings in the hall and a suspicious crackling of wrapping paper but we pretended not to notice.

It was always a shock to discover the baldy turkey laid out on the kitchen table, its head hanging down on the floor and a few drips of blood on the lino. On Christmas Eve, we crowded out on the step to hear the carol singers at the foot of the Lane, joining in the carols we knew and shouting at the other children.

'He's comin' to our house first.'

'Get away, boy; we had our chimney cleaned.'

The final ritual was when the youngest and oldest held hands to light the candle in a saucer of water. We set out a glass of porter for Santy and a slice of cake for Rudolph, urged up the stairs by Dave: 'Go on now, let ye. He'll never come if ye're awake.'

'Michael, are you still awake?'

'Yeah.'

'I tink I heard Santy.'

'Naw, boy, dat's a rat under the bed.'

I knew that was a lie. Under the bed were crates of Tanora and Little Norah and stout; there wasn't room for a rat. Still I tried to sleep in the middle of the bed hunched into the hollow of Michael's back.

It was the only morning of the year when we didn't need to be called. We were up with the light, fighting our way through the tight necks of new pullovers and racing down the stairs. The house rule was that we had to go to Mass before we opened our presents and we pressed our noses longingly to the coloured glass of the front room door, the dregs of the stout and the crumbs of cake teasing us from the table. Mass was a torture. 'If 'tis the canon, we're knackered,' Michael muttered from between latticed fingers. 'He never stops raimeishin'.' But it wasn't the canon. We barely repressed a cheer as the bustling form of Father Harte coursed the altar boy out of the sacristy. Father Harte had better sense than to preach on Christmas Day. There was a God after all.

Another of Dave's rules was that we had to stay a decent interval after the priest left the altar; then we were off like hounds from the leash, tearing up the road to rip the coloured paper to bits in a frenzy of discovery. Naturally while our hands tore at our own boxes our eyes were sizing up what the others had. Uncle Paddy always sent magic presents from America. One glorious year, there was a four-engined TWA Constellation plane for me and a helicopter for Michael. One terrible year, he got a tricycle and I got a yoke on wheels with a horse's head. I demanded a steward's inquiry, but the result stood.

'He's older than you, boy. Maybe next year Santy will bring you one.'

I wheeled my horsey to the top of the Lane and took up a position outside Barrett's door. When Michael cycled out the front door, I gave the horse his head. The fall of ground was with us and we hit the tricycle at a fair lick. The horse's head fell off and looked reproachfully at me from the concrete but the trike was wrecked. I knew they'd never lay a hand on me on Christmas Day.

Most Christmases, the only snow we got was on the Christmas cards, brittle sparkly stuff that came off on our fingers. But one year it did snow! The weather seemed to be holding its breath and there was a funny yellow glow under the clouds. Just as the streetlights lit up on Christmas Eve, the snow began to fall. Huge cotton wool flakes filled the triangle of light under the ESB pole and when we woke in the morning, the whole world had changed. In the Yard, the dustbin wore a soft white helmet crisscrossed with the filigree footprints of sparrows. Even the knobs of coal in the shed had luminous bonnets, but the clothesline was the wonder. A long slender line of snow balanced impossibly on the length of the line from end to end. Every surface was covered in white silence; even the irregular slates bumped up into rectangles, the borders around the chimneys shiny and black from the fires below.

The Quarry was a blizzard of boys and girls flaking half-made snowballs with purple fingers, noses running happily from the cold. The snowman wore Pop's soft hat and a bit of curtain material for a scarf and we checked him out the back window every night as he kept his watch. The women threw ashes in the Lane to provide a purchase but the bottom of Grawn was impassable to buses and cars, and we made a slide all the way to the cobbles at the Cathedral gate. In the first flush of enthusiasm, we went down on our bottoms, spinning wildly, our arms stretched out in exultation. Our bottoms soon froze, however; so all manner of conveyances were stolen, borrowed and invented. In the space of a single hour I saw kamikaze pilots zooming by on tomato boxes, a wheel-less pram and a young wan from Wolfe Tone Street sailing sedately in a coal scuttle. I had to settle for the turkey dish from our oven and long after dark when Dave had given up whistling from the Yard we hobbled home on numbed feet, our ears stinging from the sudden warmth of the house.

The week after that Christmas was spent playing ice hockey with hurleys and a polish tin or waiting for shawled women to pass under the laden branches of the convent trees so we could shower them with a well-lobbed snowball. We took time out to visit the cribs in the city churches, comparing them unfavourably with the one in the cathedral. 'They have a dinky donkey in Saint Mary's,' someone remarked ecumenically. 'Yeah but our baby Jesus would make bits of deres,' was the confident reply. We brought the thaw on our wellingtons in around the house and soon, too soon, the roofs were black again.

Christmas was also callers and card-games. Relations bowled in at all hours and reeled out after a sherry or whiskey from Dave's heavy hand. He had a 'pioneer's pour'.

'Aisy on, Dave; you'll have me on me ear.'

'Sure 'tis only the one day in the year.'

The hundred-and-ten was a serious business, usually played in number four where the leaves of the table were pulled out to accommodate the crowd. All the uncles, Dave, Pop, Seamus O'Brien and Dr Mack from Farna, bid and trumped well into the night. We did a tour from lap to lap, trying not to laugh as Paddy palmed the dummy hand or slipped the ace of hearts in the crack of the table for the next round. Bedtime was a movable feast because of 'the time that was in it' and one day blurred into another until the rituals of dismantling Christmas were begun. The decorations were concertina'd carefully into tins. The crib figures were laid to rest in paper habits, the lights unplugged, unstrung and coiled away. The tree, brittle now and shedding on the lino, was lifted out of the butter box and landed into the Quarry. Only the books lasted, read and reread before the fire. *Coral Island*, *Little Women*, *Kidnapped* and all the sensible presents from dutiful aunts and uncles lulled us into unaccustomed quiet wherever we could curl. The annuals were traded from one house to another, crisscrossing the smoky Lane to Mack's and Murphy's till the covers cracked and the spines gave way. I often heard adults say, 'Sure 'tis only for the children!' Not in our house, where Dave, in a new pullover, squatted on the front room floor, laying a track under arches of playing cards for a train that puffed real smoke. I remember Pop, puffing away on a new pipe, as argumentative as any child about the rules of Ludo. Years later, Dave told us of one Christmas when work was scarce and funds were low.

'On Christmas Eve, all I had left in me pocket was a shillin' for the gas and no tree bought yet. I was walking down Washington Street, wrapped up in meself, when I met Auntie Kitty. "Happy Christmas Dave," she said and pushed a ten-bob note into me pocket. Sure we were made up.'

Christmas brought out the best in them and if there was a worry about money, it was to their credit that we never knew of it. All we did know was that the fire burned brightly, the table was well laden, the visitor was welcomed night and day and we were surrounded by the secure circle of a loving tribe.

10

NEIGHBOURS

'Tis more important to have good neighbours than family
because you'll always have your neighbours.'

This was one of Dave's great proverbs and in time I
came to appreciate the truth of it. Our little ghetto was a
model of interdependence. They often said that during the
war, when tea was scarce, it wasn't unusual for our family
to make a pot of tea and another to have the leaves for
their pot. Before Nan's death, I was largely unaware of this
safety-net of lives and ties but in the shadow days that
followed, when our security lay in shreds, neighbours
were our defence against aloneness, a concrete visible
reminder of belonging.

Again it was the women who set the tone of our lives.
Any door on the Lane could be opened by a child's push
and 'bates' of bread and jam were automatically offered
and casually accepted.

Purcells' was one of my favourite ports of call. Mrs
Purcell was a widow of long-standing. She was a small
woman with grey black hair tied behind her head. She
always seemed to walk in slow motion and never passed

any remark on the small boy hovering in the hall until I took my courage to tour the laps of her grown-up children. I felt safe and accepted and ordinary in a house where I was referred to by name or as the 'child' and never as 'poor Maura's boy,' a label that marked me out as different. Even when I adventured up her steep stairs and tumbled from the top, it seemed the most natural thing in the world that I would land in Jimmy's strong arms. Mrs Purcell's affections were doled out smothered in jam or in a cup of milk from the gallon in the kitchen. Jimmy worked the night shift in Dunlop's and it was my job to hush the boys if we played outside the door. It was small recompense for the hours I spent swinging my legs under their table. Sheila and Peggy, the daughters, were fiercely protective of me, keeping sharp eyes and sharper tongues to ward off potential bullies or 'tormentors' as we called them. But my heart longed for the Christmas and summer holidays when Neilus and Chrissie, their two emigrants in England, would come home. In the absence of nephews and nieces of their own, they ruined me entirely.

Leary's was almost an extension of our own house and Eily an adopted aunt. None of us begrudged Bernie a special place in Eily's heart, knowing instinctively that even though she lavished love on Bernie, our share of her heart was undiminished. Bernie blossomed in Eily's affections and snubbed poor Jimmy Walsh for ages when he had the cheek to marry her.

In all the other houses there were children our own age and, apart from the sweat-and-blood camaraderie of hurling, there was a brisk trade in swapped comics that took us over and back the Lane. Mack's and Murphy's were bottomless wells of *Beano*s, *Dandy*s and *Beezer*s, with the occasional nugget of a sixty-four pager. I remember that most of the comics were full of war stories. All the German soldiers had square heads and only about three words of German which we included in our play. *Achtung*, *schnell* and *Kamerad* were added to our usual scripts. The Japanese soldiers had bandy legs, buck teeth and what we called City Hall glasses, round and flimsy. They had only one word between them, *banzai*, and it amazed me that they could have done so much damage working out of a vocabulary of a single word.

Through the girls, the circle widened to include the Keatings around the corner and the Ahernes in the Convent Lodge. There were only two childless houses that I can recall. A retired teacher lived on one side of us with his widowed sister. Mr Rourke was a gaunt dignified man, who made rare appearances in public. What's seldom seen in any neighbourhood generates the greatest number of stories. It seems he had our Uncle Michael in his class at one stage and when he was confounded by a sum, one evening, he knocked on Mr Rourke's door for clarification. 'The office is closed,' was the response and the door closed definitively. I remember him as a man who would sometimes appear at the door to the front room when we were hunkered over our homework at the table. 'Twould halt your heart to look up from an Irish book and see this apparition framed in the doorway, a top-coat draped like a cloak over his shoulders. 'The ghost who walks,' Michael whispered one evening, and earned a look from Dave.

'Good evening, Dave.'

'Good evening and welcome, Mr Rourke; will you sit up to the fire?'

'No thank you, Dave, [he never did] I have a little message for these miscreants.' Then he'd open his coat dramatically and all the rubber balls that had been 'banished' into his yard from the Quarry would bounce merrily around our front room. After he died, his sister gave us a set of encyclopedias from his collection of books. For years after, it mopped up the boredom of many a wet day and added an exotic spice to our school essays.

Even though she was no relation, we called his sister Auntie. It was the accepted thing that we would pause in our game, and 'hold up the ball' to let Auntie pass in safety. Someone would always take her string bag of messages as she struggled up Saint Mary's Road under her black shawl. We weren't as eager to enter her house, because we had invested it with ghosts and phantoms to match the noises that came through our bedroom wall at night. Auntie would get lonesome some nights and take consolation in a Baby Power. At some stage during the night, she'd part company with the bed and call out to Dave for help. In the first stages of sleep, we'd hear her thin voice, muffled by the wall.

'Dave! Dave!'

'Dad!'

'Wha'?'

'I think Auntie's callin' ya.'

Without complaint, he'd hoist his trousers over his pyjamas and stumble off to the rescue. She was nearly the death of him. He told us how accustomed he got to lifting her off the floor in the gloomy house and tucking her into the bed like a child.

'Sure there was no weight in her and I was half asleep meself. Then I'd sit down on a chair and wait for her to nod off. Well one night I'm sittin' there on me own and ye know how dark 'twas. "David," she says, as clear as a bell, "you may go home to your own house now, boy, because my father has just come in to keep me company." The hairs on the back of me neck stood up to attention.'

Worse was to follow. As he felt his way carefully down the rickety stairs in pitch darkness, he distinctly heard a tapping sound follow his every step.

'When I got to the end of the stairs, I was in a bog of sweat. I went in me own door like a greyhound.'

And, though we had heard it over and over, we supplied his cue.

'And what was it, Dad?'

'Yerra, 'twas me braces hangin' down behind me.'

Twice a day, Bridgie's house was awash with children, and none of them her own. Bridgie had converted her house on Saint Mary's Road into a small shop and the house speciality was toffee. This was boiled up on the stove in the kitchen and poured out on a slab to cool into a brittle glacier. She hammered it into small crazy-paving pieces and packed them in a twist of paper for a penny. She was tall and gangly and an expert on crowd control. 'If you don't stop your pushin' I'll tell the teacher.' This put immediate manners on the pusher because everyone knew that Bridgie had a great leg of the nuns. In the summer, the school market dried up totally and Bridgie kept the shop open for company. I became a regular caller during the long summer evenings. I'd rap on the wall beside the curtained door to her inner sanctum.

'Are you there, Bridgie?'

'Where else would I be! Come in and let me look at you.'

'I was wonderin' if you wanted any messages?'

'No, sit down there for a minute.'

Sometimes, she was sitting up in the bed with her crochet needle flying, surrounded by a whirlpool of coloured threads and patches. Behind her on the wall over the mantelpiece she had a framed picture crowded with cameos of the leaders of the Rising. The only one I could recognise straight away was Padraig Pearse because he had his head turned sideways. 'That was because he had a squinty eye,' someone said irreverently at home. 'Wasn't he very vain all the same?' Instinctively, I kept that particular insight to myself. Occasionally, Bridgie liked to 'tour' the picture, giving a running commentary on her heroes.

'Dere's Connolly at the top, mud fat with a tash. Never darkened the door of church or chapel,' she sniffed. 'And dat mawkish lookin' fella was Plunkett, writin' poetry God help us and the GPO burnin' around him.' Another sniff. In Bridgie's world order, missing Mass and writing poetry were reserved sins. She would meander down the picture as I sat, half shocked and totally fascinated by the contrast between Bridgie's version and the blood and glory stories we were fed at school.

Another evening, it would be 'de Tans'.

'De sweepins of English jails, boy, roamin' de streets of Cork in their tenders, puttin' the fear of God into innocent people. But dey got deir lot from our boys down here,' she'd say with satisfaction, stabbing the needle into the innocent ball of wool. I held my breath, wishing her on to the gory bits. Pop had fought the Tans and sometimes could be wheedled into stories. But they were all about nicknames, and burying rifles up the Brake. Eventually I'd lose patience with him and blurt out the important question:

'Did you shoot anyone, Pop?'

'Tis very late,' he'd say. 'Yeer father will be wonderin'.' Having fought against them he had to go and make his living among them in the Dagenham foundry. During his exile, he developed a great respect for what he called 'the real English people' as he huddled into basements with them from Hitler's bombs. Bridgie had no such brakes.

'Dere was terrible bad tings done too, boy. A gang of de boys shot an informer over the road dere one night, and, God forgive them, wasn't he out of his mind with drink.'

She stopped, and looked beyond me and the sweet-smelling shop to hard and hurtful times.

Bridgie was the only one who spoke easily about Maura, my mother. She could switch with stomach-wrenching suddenness from an ambush to something Maura said to her on the road or a dress she had worn on a summer's evening. I sat there trying to be invisible, gathering these throwaway threads and weaving them into the sepia-coloured memory I carried in my heart.

'Wait till your father comes home,' was a common threat in the Lane. I never appreciated that men who were gone to work before we opened our eyes and came home, tired in the evenings, got the short end of the stick by being cast in the role of the heavy hand of justice. I remember them as *Echo*-readers, kindly men who tossed my hair and said things like: 'You're gettin' very lanky, God bless ya!' or 'What book are you in now?' The Mack's dad was a foreman carpenter and clerk of works on the new church at the top of Grawn. Neilus's dad worked in Goulding's fertiliser factory out in the Glen. He let us see the vats of acid one day and lit a match by touching it to the surface of the innocent-looking liquid. His shirt had lots of tiny holes burned into it by the splatters from the vats.

Only two men didn't go to regular jobs. Thomas lived alone and rarely spoke to anyone but that 'was his way,' and no one passed any remark on him. Mrs Purcell made sure the gasman had access to the meter and his sister came once a week to tidy the house for him. Jack, the other one, had a hump on his back, a permanent cap and a passion for opera. Dave swore that Jack could have been on the stage of the Opera House 'if 'twasn't for his affliction.' Passing Keatings' door was an education as Gigli and Tauber swelled out of the house from his scratchy records. When Jack took a notion to cut sticks for his mother in the backyard, the neighbourhood men would take the *Echo* to the outside toilets to enjoy the arias in doubtful Italian that poured pure and strong from his twisted body.

The two men who were the supports of our world lived just two doors apart. Pop, my grandfather, smelled of pipe tobacco and trained me as his acolyte. I would take the moist plug in my left hand and the shiny silver knife in my right. 'Mind your fingers, for the love of God.' The whittled grains had to be rubbed into curls in my palm before they were mixed with the 'dottle' from the previous smoke. This dusty concoction was tamped firmly into the bowl and at last the match was struck. 'Always strike away from yourself, boy, in case the sulphur flies.' It was vital to keep the match away from the bowl until the sulphur burned away and then it had to be held over the bowl so that the flame was drawn into the tobacco. When this painstaking ritual was finally completed, he'd puff furiously for a few seconds – and the pipe would go out. 'Arrah, bad cess to it,' he'd say good humouredly, 'but the fella who invented the pipe wanted to sell matches.'

He was also my tutor in the mysteries of one-hundred-and-ten, dealing the hands on a chair set between the two of us before the fire. 'Five, Jack, Joker, Ace of Hearts, Ace of Trumps, highest in red, lowest in black,' I recited to his satisfaction at the end of our first lesson. I learned to hold my cards well up to my chest, to 'poke' against the dealer with a handy trump and never ever to renege. The cards were an excuse for talk about promising terriers and famous hounds, and a closeness grew between us until the night he broke the rules. 'C'mere,' I said, 'you reneged on my Ace of Hearts.' The apprentice had dared to question the master. He looked at me over the tops of his glasses. 'I did not.' But I was like a Jack Russell in a ditch, answering to no master in my pursuit of prey. It ended badly. 'Well,' I said righteously, 'if that's the way you're going to play, I won't play at all.' I stormed out the door to my own house. Dave could read me like a book. 'What happened?' I related my tale, a little less assured now that my *teaspach* had worn off. 'Go up now.

ye caffler, and apologise to Pop.' It was the longest walk of my life. By the time I got to his door, my eyes were dangerously full. He was sitting where I had left him, the pipe going full blast, the cards untouched. ''Tis your deal' he said, before I could open my mouth, saving me the shame and scald of tears. We played on far into the evening as if nothing had happened between us. He had great nature in him and I loved him fiercely for it.

Dave ordered our evenings around the homework. He had a great belief that 'de books' would be our passport to good jobs and a better life. He hovered over us as we wrestled with sums which he had a gift for and Irish which he couldn't fathom at all. Kay was our reference point when deciding whether there was or wasn't a *séimhiú*. The wonder was that she ever got her own work done between us.

With the books away in the sacks at last, we would have a concert. The small hall off the kitchen had a curtain to catch the draught from the back door and we took turns before it, announcing the acts into the handle of the brush.

'And now, ladies and gentlemen, Bernie Kenneally.'

Loud applause from the audience as Bernie entangles herself in the curtain and then escapes to stand scarlet beside the gas-stove. 'A bit of order now,' Dave commanded the unruly crowd in the gods. 'Now, Ber girl.' In her small tuneless voice she would start into 'Every lickle girl would like to be . . . ' Michael and I would be bent double in an agony of giggles.

'I'll soften the two of ye. Go on girl, don't mind them.' Michael and I sang a duet we entitled 'Off with the boys on an engine' and Kay sang 'De swallow now.' Maybe the same scene was being reenacted in the other houses up and down the Lane but nowhere with such energy and abandon, as if we had to try harder to keep the shadows at bay and fill the empty places. Reluctantly we set the table for the night supper and vied for Dave's lap as he sang in a sweet tenor voice,

> Oh my baby, my curly headed baby,
> Your Daddy's workin' in de cotton fields;
> He's workin' dere for you.

This was the promise that would lull us up the stairs, knowing that he would be there if we called out during the night, waking from a dream, or just to check that we weren't alone.

'Dad.'

'What, boy?'

'Nothing.'

'All right, off to sleep now, 'tis very late.'

11

THE SEASIDE

We all went down to Youghal.
We let the baby fall.
Me mother came out
and gave me a clout
and turned me into
a bottle of stout.

It wasn't Shakespeare but that popular ditty perfectly expressed the madness, the sheer self-abandonment that infected us at the mention of Youghal. As city children we rarely ran for more than twenty yards in a straight line. There was always some obstruction, human or man-made, that turned us jinking left and right like swallows. We seldom settled into the exultation of free flight. Youghal was a massive open space with an alarming expanse of sky. The mysterious sea stretched out and up to meet the sky without the blinkers of city walls.

The adults packed as if we were going to America, lumbering themselves with pannier bags of sandwiches and changes of clothing. These were carefully folded for children who would live in a togs for the day. We walked *en masse* to the railway station, savouring the soot and smoke smell, clinging close against the squeal of coupling carriages. At last in a sudden snort of steam we were off. The train grumbled and complained down the line to Dunkettle, picked up speed as we flashed by Midleton and tore through the sedate rich fields of East Cork, a scarf of smoke waving over its shoulder. We roared from the windows at bemused cattle and screamed under bridges, ignoring the order to 'come in outta dat; ye'll get smuts in yer eyes', vying with each other to be the first to spot the pale blue rim of the sea.

Outside Youghal station, we clambered up the sharp-grassed sand dunes and stopped at the top, overawed by the immensity before us. After much deliberation, the adults eventually agreed on a spot with 'a bit of shelter', where they spread the blanket and anchored the bags. Pop's concession to the seaside was to roll up the legs of his trousers and drape a hanky over his head. Nelly, dressed in black, sat erect and unmoving, her pale face tilted up to the sun. Dave fretted at the notion of sitting on a patch of sand and wandered off on bare snow-white feet in search of shells and stones.

We hopped from foot to foot, dragging off our clothes, whinging when a lace wouldn't loosen, mewling like pups in a cage until we were free. The first moments were heady and unforgettable. Running full tilt on the firm wet sand, we held our arms outstretched, mimicking the wheeling gulls, before we hit the water. I pranced in to the depth of my knees and thought better of it, contenting myself with racing sideways in shin-deep water, holding imaginary reins in one hand and slapping my backside with the other. It was a day outside time when we wandered back to the blanket at will for cup or crust, our eyes roving over our shoulders all the while, impatient for adventure.

Halfway up the beach one day, I found half a dozen mackerel floating in the water, a loop of twine through their gills. I couldn't believe my good fortune. These were the prized fish that sometimes sizzled on our pan in a sea of molten butter and God had gifted me with six of them. My return to the blanket was a slow and studied triumph. Men with red faces and women with red chests over cotton frocks called out from the blankets.

'Young fella, where did'ya get dem fish?'

'Back dere.'

I nodded nonchalantly behind me. In my wake children were shanghaied into going back the strand to buy the tea. My own crowd were less enthusiastic.

'God knows where they came from. Wouldn't you throw them back like a good boy?'

I wouldn't and didn't. No amount of cajoling or threats could stir me from my resolve to bring the fish home and re-enact my glory in the Lane. I hid them in a hollow behind the sand dunes and whiled away the day building sandcastles and burying Bernie. Finally, we tiptoed up the cooling sands, lips blue and teeth chattering, to a huddle of towels and the tired trek to the train.

In latter years, Dave recalled what happened then.

'Dem bloody fish were a mixed blessing. Dey were as high as kites so we had a carriage to ourselves and we had to take turns putting our heads out the window for air.'

Uncle Christy had summed up an individual one time by remarking that parts of him had died years before. God alone knew when these fish had died but their stench filled the carriage. Dave and Pop were throwing dangerous eyes at them but I threatened to make a disgrace of them and they kept their distance. We cut a swathe through the crowds in the Cork Station, the fish held out before me like Moses's staff over the Red Sea. Nelly prevailed where all the others failed. Outside the Coliseum Cinema in MacCurtain Street, she asked me very quietly if I would 'throw them away, alanna, 'cos they'll bring a fit of sickness into the house.' My stubbornness, which had stiffened against the threats of the men, melted away under her soft gaze, and the fish fell at the side of the road. I thought their eyes looked up reproachfully at me from the rubbish.

Crosshaven was a different experience altogether. It is a small village tucked into the elbow of the estuary, just around the corner from the sea. Spike Island is the centre hub of the vast circle of water that separates brash Crosshaven from the stolid cathedral town of Cobh. The twin arms of the harbour extend to Roche's Point on the Cobh side and Church Bay on the other. They are straddled by two large navy forts. The one on the Crosshaven side is called Camden, and it hulks over the harbour under a camouflage of scrub grass and gorse. The stretch of rocks and small bays snaking to the sea from the foot of Camden was the Corkman's Costa del Sol.

I went there just once on a northside expedition, organised by Auntie Nell and Auntie Noreen. The troop who pitched camp in a tiny bungalow on a bend in the boreen above Graball Bay also included Auntie Eily, Kay, Bernie, Michael, Auntie Noreen, her husband Sean, their baby Brenda and myself. The bungalow was so small that when Eily asked a fella she had met on the beach up for tea, he said he'd leave his bike in the shed. Mortified, she had to explain that the shed was our bungalow. There were two beds in the inside room. Noreen and Sean had one and the rest crowded into the other. When they were all safely installed, Sean pulled the high pram in behind them. Michael and I slept on air beds on the kitchen floor. The last ritual every night was blowing up the beds and climbing in to sleep with the aftertaste of rubber on our tongues. The beds must have had a slow leak for halfway through the night the cold of the floor brought me awake and Michael was in the same predicament. I sat up in the dark and clocked myself on the open door of the dresser. 'Jesus Mary and Joseph,' Auntie Nelly exclaimed from the inside room, 'we have burglars in the bungalow.'

'Auntie Nelly,' I called out plaintively, 'our beds are after going down.'

In blessed relief, Auntie Nelly started to laugh. That drove me mad altogether, so I added, 'And I'm after clocking meself on the dresser.' That set the rest of them off. Brenda, who was normally a placid child, woke up and started to give tongue. That set them shrieking and gasping. 'Where's Auntie Nelly gone?' Kay asked in the middle of the racket. 'I'm here girl, under Eily.' The little wooden bungalow seemed to rock and sway with the force of their laughter. Despite my self-pity, it was a moment I would never forget. Their laughter teased me into good form again, and, without further grumbling, I blew up my bed, every puff fanning fresh gales of laughter from the women. I pulled it away from the murderous dresser and settled down again, ready to add my own three halfpence to the fun.

'Burglars? Sure there's no room to break in here.'

At that stage, Nelly took a fit of coughing and that put a halt to our gallop. At last, I went to sleep, satisfied with the thought that Michael, as usual, would remember nothing in the morning and I could add legs to the story without fear of contradiction.

Almost every other year, I went to Crosshaven with my southside Auntie Nora, who was a demon for it. Nora was a small, bird-like woman with dancing eyes and a great tongue for slagging. Whenever Dave trooped us over her threshold for a visit, she'd cry out in mock horror, 'Hide de bird; dey're here from the northside.' Despite the fact that her two girls went to Saint Al's school, which we thought snobby, and her two boys favoured Sully's Quay, our mortal hurling enemies, we were the best of friends.

They lived in a house that hung precariously to the foot of the Barrack wall, overlooking the South channel of the river. Kyser's Hill was a cliff of steps leading to their front door, and the air was always spicy with the combined smells of the Mills and Beamish's brewery. Their father, John Scannell, was a small stocky man of massive dignity. He was a builder who laid floors, dashed walls and mended roofs and so, the northsiders claimed, Nora prayed for storms. John had two worker/acolytes called Willie and Jimmy who always cycled the requisite bike length behind their boss or manoeuvred the hand-truck laden with ladders called 'the iron maiden.' His own house was a collection of architectural afterthoughts, dropping from a high front door down two steep steps to a meandering hall that wound out and up to a back kitchen hanging out over a quarry. It was a warm welcoming house polished to a glow by Nora's mop and bucket. As soon as summer warmed the Barrack wall, the swallows flew in from Capistrano and Nora flew out to Crosshaven.

She always invited me for a fortnight and then forgot I was there for about five weeks. We had different bungalows over the years on the hill above Graball Bay but the most memorable was a lean-to affair, grafted on to the side of a family home. The proprietors were called Heaps and they had a sign hanging out on the fuchsia hedge advertising 'Boiling Water'. This was a great challenge to our creative skills and we'd drive them mad, skipping in and out of the yard singing, 'Boiling water, pots of tea, made from Mrs Heaps' wee wee.'

The Crosshaven shoreline was a relief after the dizzying spaces of Youghal. Fingers of rock stuck out from the cliffs, carving the beach into hundreds of small cosy places, perfectly comfortable for families accustomed to the confines of two-up two-down houses. Nervous of the water, and influenced by Dave's yen for discovery, the stretch from Camden to Church Bay became my area of adventure. Nora never minded what time we fell out of the beds. Breakfast was a casual cup of tea and a bite of whatever was going. Then I was off on a lone voyage. Rock pools were a rich seam that took hours to mine. I would smash a barnacle on a rock and peel out the flat leathery creature, rinsing away the yellow stuff in salt water. A

length of twine, weighted by a stone, with the barnacle
bait tied on at the end and I was crab fishing. The trick
was to lower the bait close to the foot of the rock and
watch it wave tantalisingly to and fro 'til the crab scuttled
out and grabbed it. Then slowly, very slowly, I would haul
the prize up on to the rock. I was much too cautious to
chance my fingers against his pincers and usually hoofed
him back into the water. The pools had their share of
small crabs with flaps on their bellies that we called
purses. Bloodshot anemones waved their hairy heads,
sifting the water for food. I often obliged them whenever
sprats did a kamikaze on the beach, pursued by mackerel.
Any flicker of a rockfish meant hours of bailing with a
tin can just to hold the wriggler by the tail for a few
seconds. The shark was a shock.

I was sitting under Camden, on a warm and reasonably
ridge-free slab of rock, resting from my labours at the
rock pool. The slow green swell had lulled me into a
daydream when a sleek grey shape slid from the corner
of my eye into full focus. The perfect creature turned
lazily in an impossible space and was gone again. I
remember a feeling of exhilaration spread out from my
stomach, as if the sea had singled me out, a child of the
shallows, to experience something special from the deep.
I never told a single soul. Partly because I didn't want to
risk a slagging but mostly because I thought the magic
might be diluted in the telling.

To Nora's eternal credit, she never stood in my light
or limited my scope with expectations of playing with the
others or staying within sight of the blanket on the
strand. I remember when Dave visited she said, 'I never

see that child from one end of the day to the other.' She said it in a tone of acceptance rather than of accusation and I felt grateful to her. There was a healing in the long lone hours scaling warm rocks, and comfort in the regular inhale/exhale of the tide that loosened old knots and made me, for a time, carefree.

The estuary was always busy with boats. Small trawlers could be seen in the early morning swell, appearing and disappearing in the waves, pushing for the fishing grounds beyond Daunt's Rock. Petrol tankers seemed to have only a front and aft, their low-slung bellies invisible from the shore. I got used to the passage of high and low boats, only occasionally pausing from play to watch a navy corvette, grey and purposeful, slicing out the bay. One ship was different to all the others. I remember watching its passage in silence, allowing it the respectful pause from play we gave the Angelus. The *Inisfallen* was well-known to all Cork people. Over the years, it had carried someone from every northside family to exile in England. Some returned and some didn't, and this potential for bereavement froze the walkers on the cliffs as the gulls keened behind the massed decks of the black and white ship.

Wet days were a killer, whiled away with card games on the lino between the bunks. The hours were marked off by the mournful bellow of the foghorn from Roche's Point. Fog settled like a suffocating facecloth over the bungalow, erasing the ditch at the foot of the garden. The light outside was headachy bright as the sun fought loyally to burn our mood away. By the second day cabin fever was rife and petty fights broke out over what was trumps and we were banished to the bunks to brood through books we'd read already. Hutchie's father broke the spell. 'Awful day, missus,' was his passport to the teapot.

'Desperate, boy! I'm driven demented.'

'Sure I know, me own crowd are like a parcel of cats. Listen, boys: I have news for ye. Accordin' to the paper, there's a liner due in tomorrow mornin'. About half five she's due.'

Despite the weight of the fog, our gloom lifted. A liner, Janey Mack.

The following morning we tiptoed out the door, catching it before it could lash back on its spring and wake the house. Graball Bay was mysterious with fog and the tolling of invisible buoys. There was a grassy hollow half way over the cliff and we hunched there, miserable with damp. Then as if in answer to our unspoken prayers the fog rolled up and a city of lights appeared before us, floating on throbbing engines up the channel to Cobh. Our hearts beat in sympathetic rhythm as this apparition from another world eased slowly out of sight, only the high breakers on the strand beneath convincing us that it hadn't been a dream.

In Crosshaven, the day belonged to the sea and the night belonged to the merries. At the start of every holiday, I measured out my money for the merries. There might be the odd lop (penny) for a few sweets or an extravagant threepence for an ice-cream, but the merries merited a full shilling for every night of the week. When the tea was over, we quelled our impatience, kicking a ball outside the bungalow until Nora wheeled out the go-car.

At the first bend of the road, beyond Driscolls' farm, we cut across country, along the flank of the cross-topped hill and quickened our pace with the fall of ground to the lights below. The merries spun and sparkled to loud music behind a whitewashed wall. Trailers and generators formed a rough square, and, as daylight ebbed to stars, this was our patch of magic.

We were spoiled for choice. The swinging boats had the double advantage of being cheap and not too adventurous. There was also a fair chance that the man would get forgetful about regular customers and we'd have two or three gos for our money, before he'd raise the plank and judder us back to earth. We became expert at timing the pull on the downswing for maximum lift and raising our bottoms to avoid the friction from the plank. The bumpers were mostly a spectator sport. We thrilled to the whine of the engines as they charged about under their pilot light spark and held our breath as the attendants rode the rubber rims to turn the wheel for helpless girls. But we watched our chance and sometimes approached a lone grown-up.

'Can I go round with you, sir?'

This gambit worked wonders on fellas with new long pants and pimples who didn't have to pay for the passenger anyway. For the next frantic five minutes I would clutch the rim, pretending to steer Mick Scannell's bumper into the retaining border, all the while changing gear and revving in my throat.

The large wheel that loomed high above the merries made me dizzy looking at it so I gave it a wide berth. A sawn-off, butty little man in a posh waistcoat took bets on metal coloured horses that ran round a turntable on his stall. Tuppence on the right horse could boost our stock to a full shilling. If Mamie was with us, we were made. She spent her whole night on the wheel of fortune and never came away without cups and saucers or, if we could get to her on time, a football. It was usually a light plastic one that put up with a few kicks on the strand before it headed for England on an off-shore breeze.

No night in the merries was complete without chips. The chip shop was strategically placed right opposite the entrance and had seduced our noses long before our bellies urged us out. It was always boiling with people. The ageless woman behind the counter shovelled, bagged and shook salt and vinegar in one smooth movement, shelling change and shouting orders all the time. Out of good manners, we offered a chip to the adults and happily they rarely accepted. This was the feast for the road home, to be eaten with mouths opened wide for relief from the scald of salty chips. It was always with a sense of disappointment that we groped our way to the crunchy bits of flotsam swimming in vinegar at the bottom of the bag. Night supper was a cup of milky tea and talking softly so as not to wake Catherine and Gerard. Mamie and Nora, freed from the laundry and the house on Kyser's Hill, swapped stories over and back about that foreign country, the southside, answering the questions in my head about the other half of my tribe. At last the beds and the final satisfaction of putting my feet on Mick Scannell's sunburn before the memories of treasure pools and rhythmic waves lulled me off to sleep.

12

ALTAR BOYS

In our Lane the only kind of boy to be was a Mon boy.
The North Mon was where big boys went after their first
holy communion to play hurling, be taught by 'de monks'
and get good jobs. That was the dream of parents who
had never gone there themselves but who would put up
with any hardship to make sure their children did. Like
all traditions it had its private and public heroes. Our
uncles had all soldiered there and hadn't Jack Lynch been
a Mon boy himself. But first, there was the hurdle of first
communion.

Sister Eucharia chanted us through our prayers and
tapped a spoon on our tongues in the nun's chapel to
prepare us for the day. The more delicate among us had
qualms about being down the queue for the spoon.
Nobody wanted to be behind Whacker, convinced he had
the mange at least and the spoon would give us 'a fit of
the gawks'. Communion was preceded by confession and
it was a shock to discover that most of what we had done
for the past seven years was a sin. There was also a
serious practical problem. How could we do a reasonable

stocktake of seven years' blackguarding in just a few minutes? I settled on a formula that stood me in good stead for years. 'I told lies; I didn't do what I was told; I threw stones; I back-answered me father.' Three Hail Marys was a fair penance for that list of misdemeanours. Some of the desperadoes in my class had more serious matters to confess.

'I stole a Woodbine from me Daddy's box.'

'I kept the change from the messages.'

'I put pepper in me Nanny's snuff.'

The prospect quietened them for weeks before the event. On the dreaded day we were shepherded up Gerald Griffin Street by Sister Eucharia into the candle-flecked gloom of the North chapel. I had my fingers crossed that I'd get either Father Harte or Father O'Sullivan. They were pushovers when it came to penance and my prayers were answered. Other 'seeds fell among thorns'. In some of the other boxes, there were a few red faces, the odd tear and one or two puddles of perfect contrition.

The communion suit was got from a tailor in Castle Street. Pop and Dave nodded approvingly while a small fidgety man made me nervous sticking and slashing with pins and chalk. It was a good suit but not a miraculous one like Michael's. My brother's communion coincided with bad times at the factory. Dave was working some days and 'idle' more. Nan had worried about the expense of the suit and took the worry to her prayers at the side of her bed. 'During the night I opened me eyes and there was Maura. "Mother," she said, "you'll find the money for the suit in the leaves of the front-room table."' Over a cup of tea the following morning Nan shared the apparition with Auntie Noreen and the two of them ventured to the front room. 'When I tugged at the table, didn't a roll of notes drop at me feet on the floor.' My communion was not as dramatic but just as rewarding financially. After the tour of the tribe I had a satisfying crackle in every pocket of the new suit.

In a fit of religious zeal, I decided I wanted to be an altar boy. 'Well, your brother is a very good altar boy,' said Father Cashman. 'He's always on time for the early Mass. I hope you'll be just as good.' I didn't point out that Michael's punctuality had more than a little to do with Dave's threat to 'flake the backside off him' if he didn't get out of the bed.

Nelly and Noreen brought me up to the Good Shepherd Convent in Sunday's Well to be fitted for an altar boy's outfit. I wasn't too mad about that idea because the Good Shepherd nuns ran an orphanage and we were regularly threatened with it when we were bold. The altar boy's 'togs' was made up of a long purple soutane with too many buttons, and a snow-white surplice to put over it. This was topped off with a scarlet cape that went around the shoulders and was fastened with a hook and eye under the chin. We wore knee-length scarlet socks that could double as football socks and a pair of black 'rubber dollies'. The interesting thing about Mass at that time was that nobody understood a single word of it. Apart from the sermon and the announcements it was in Latin. The congregation usually rattled their beads or read their prayer books and left everything else to the priest and altar boys, who had their backs turned to the congreg-ation to 'keep their business to themselves'. Father

Cashman was a slim, slow-moving man with high eyebrows and a beautiful singing voice. He was another one who should 'have been in the Opera House,' according to Dave. He was firm but kindly and explained the words carefully as he went along. I was fascinated by the long musical sounds and began to pick it up fairly fast, aided by tutorials from Michael at home.

'What are the two of ye doin' with the good cloth off the table?'

'We're practising Benediction.'

'I'll bless yeer backsides with the brush, if ye don't go out and play.'

The Latin did nothing for Towser. ''Tis all double Dutch to me, boy' he confided one Monday evening before Father Cashman came for the lesson. 'It's easy!' I said innocently. 'When the priest turns around and says, "*Dominus Vobiscum*" we have to say, "*Et cum spiritu tuo.*" Towser went into convulsions. 'Lads, d'ye hear dis?' He turned to his eager audience and spread his arms. 'Dominic, did de biscuits come?' Then he joined them reverently for the reply. 'Yes, but father, I got none.' Pandemonium broke loose in the presbytery room till one of the priest's housekeepers put her head in the door and snarled us into silence.

Father Cashman trained us to genuflect without falling over and to strike the consecration bell a glancing bow with the padded side of the stick. For our inaugural flights, he apprenticed us to the big fellas. 'Whatever they do, let ye do too,' was his final word. With this motto emblazoned on our hearts, we dogged the footsteps of the regulars. Michael glanced down the bench one evening during Benediction at David McGrath who was picking his nose. 'Hey, sham, cut that out.'

'But you were doing it,' came the indignant reply. Another evening, one of the old stagers was short-taken during a long sermon to the women's confraternity. With all the self-conscious grace of an ambitious monsignor, he genuflected before the high altar and made his escape to the waste ground at the side of the chapel. He was standing there with his soutane hoisted, tracing his initials on the wall, when a sudden premonition made him wheel round. Two small altar boys were standing behind him, their hands joined perfectly before them.

Most of us managed some semblance of grace and composure on the altar but Theo had an extra elbow and no coordination. Every time he came out to light the candles, he clattered the sanctuary lamp with the taper. His most effective method of quenching candles was to knock them. Towser kept up a commentary from the benches: 'Four down and comin' into de straight. Can he make it a full house?' Theo poured the cruets up the priest's sleeve, banged the communicants under the chin with the paten and got a bong from the bell that was painful. 'D'ye know,' Michael observed wisely, 'I'd say he's drainin' the wine cruet.' It wasn't unheard of and some fellas took a terrible chance blowing out the candles.

The new bishop was Dr Lucey and he said the eight o'clock Mass in our chapel every Sunday. He was a slight man with a pale face and black eyes thatched thickly with enormous eyebrows. We waited inside the sacristy door to slobber all over his ring when he arrived to vest. Adults seemed to go stiff and awkward in his presence but we were easy with him, sensing that underneath the ascetic exterior he had a warm heart. Sometimes he'd prod us into telling stories from school and shock the priests with a burst of laughter. On one such occasion, an old neighbour completely forgot herself. She touched him gently on the arm and said, 'C'mere, me lord. You should laugh more often, it takes years off ya.'

Some of the priests we admired for their sanctity and some for their humanity, and a few we revered because they managed to combine both. Father Harte was my favourite. He had a red face, topped by a head of hair the colour of a rusty Brillo pad. He had the temper to match his colouring and could deliver a clip to a rubber-necking altar-boy that would 'soften his cough for him'. But we saw his kindness and patience with the old people and the effort he put into the Mass, and felt comfortable in the company of a truly holy man.

The women of the parish flocked to Father Jerry's confession box. Auntie Nelly swore by him.

'If you told dat man you were after murderin' your husband, he'd say, sure you didn't mean it darlin'.'

Nearly all of our priests were bony farmers' sons from West Cork and coming to our parish must have been a terrible shock to their systems. For one thing, there was the language problem. On any Saturday night in the box they could hear that someone had been 'connyshurin'', 'doin' a foxer' or 'slockin' and with the secrecy of the confessional, who could they ask for translations? The majority, very wisely, opted for the most charitable interpretation and were acclaimed for their understanding. Small wonder then, that one little woman who had appeared stricken before going into the box, bounced out with a light step and a broad smile. In a loud whisper, she confided the source of her happiness to her pal: 'He's in from the country, girl. Sure he haven't a gowries, tank God.'

Over the years priests came and went but there was one special man who stayed and had a profound effect on generations of altar boys. Paddy Dwyer had all the best virtues of the priesthood and none of the power. He was known throughout the northside as Paddy the clerk. Paddy was the man who arrived at first light from his home in O'Connell Street. He unlocked the church, hung up his coat and hat and put on his vestments for the day. With his grizzled grey-black hair and big build, he was an impressive figure in his spotless black soutane. Paddy's breviary was the *Cork Examiner* and the first altar boy through the door every morning was dispatched to Statia Cahill's to buy it. I always tried to be the messenger because there was a tanner in it. He would lay it out on the big bench in the sacristy and as I dressed in the altar-boys passageway I'd hear his prayers: 'Well, my God, hah. This fella wasn't at the same match at all.' In preparation for the priest, he laid out the flat dalmatic and pooled the alb, curling the cincture in two perfect loops so that the tassels hung straight. Lastly, he placed the stole in a perfect inverted vee and draped it with the amice. He went through that ritual many times every day and I never recall him touching and folding with anything but gentle reverence. Certificates of baptisms and marriages, Mass cards for a coffin, palms for pictures and ashes for foreheads as well as unruly altar boys were all part of his function. Sometimes, in the evening, he would kneel up on the bench that ran under the window and with his elbows on the sill watch the passage of people in Roman Street. He was a man who noticed and pondered. 'D'ye know, boy,' he said to me once, 'I saw a marvellous thing today. We had two coffins down at the back of the church and one of them was covered in Mass cards. The other poor craythur was from one of the Lanes and hadn't chick nor child. Well, I declare to God but after the ten o'clock Mass, wasn't there a procession to the door of people looking to have Mass cards signed for the bare coffin. Isn't there great nature in people all the same!'

In the summer we made a fortune from the weddings. After the Mass we'd invent reasons to hang around the sacristy until the best man got the message. The other perks of the job were ringing the Angelus bell for sixpence and going to a Presentation Brother's funeral at the top of Blarney Street. The Brothers always gave a party for the altar boys after the burial and I firmly believe we decimated the Order with our prayers for their happy release.

The mission was always standing room only. Fellas who owed their religious allegiance to the Harrier Bar and Flaherty's pub all year pooled self-consciously around the chapel doors and spilled into the seats at the last stroke of the bell. This was the only time in the year that we had to leave the altar for the sermon, under strict instructions from Paddy to be back in time for Benediction. With the thundering roar of 'We Stand for God' in our ears, we scampered down to the opposition. Shandon Steeple looked disdainfully down on Dominic Street and between the steeple and its graveyard, there was a perfect place for soccer. Someone always had to keep an eye on the Shandon's clock in case we missed our duty, but Shandon had four clocks that often disagreed. It was known to the locals as the 'four-faced liar'. At the last minute we'd burst into the sacristy and drag on our togs in the passageway that smelled of socks and incense. Then we'd bustle out the door to the altar before the missioner who was cloaked in gold for Benediction. We got some funny looks from the priests but none of them ever queried our sweaty faces. Maybe they took our flushed appearance as a compliment to their preaching or as a kind of solidarity with the fellas sweating in the seats below.

Characters and crying children were things we took for granted. Visiting priests would startle to hear a loud voice from the back of the church roaring 'Holy Mary, Mudder o' God . . . ' We never turned a hair; sure 'twas only Dinny Daly. To ring the Mass bell, we had to manoeuvre around Dan at the foot of the stairs. A deaf mute, he would mime his frantic Mass, the cap stuck like a biretta on his bald head. Dogs were regular Massgoers, only ejected by a wary altar boy when they got too ambitious and wandered inside the rails. Jenny's dog was always in the chapel. He sat devoutly at her feet through three Masses and was often pointed out as an example to fidgety children. One night, he took a turn for the worst and laced into Jim Keating at devotions. Poor Jenny was covered with confusion. 'You'll have to excuse him, Jim,' she said apologetically. 'Tis his first time doing the Stations.'

13

ENDINGS

The North Mon primary school was bright and busy and 'de monks' weren't the ogres the older ones had promised. Brother McCormick was a 'new' monk, fresh and lively, enthusiastically coaxing us through our Irish and driven to despair by my handwriting. 'Maybe you'll be a doctor, boy,' he said hopefully. But despite my leaning scrawl, I loved the challenge of new words and the complexity of fractions. We came across the word 'brazier' one day in our reading book.

'Boys, who can pronounce that word for me?'

'Brudder, brudder.'

For once, my hand caught his eye.

'Yes, Christy.'

'Brudder, brassiere, brudder.'

He had to threaten them with the leather to still their roars.

We graduated from Brother McCormick to Mr O'Sullivan. He was a small excitable man with a high colour and thick glasses, who placed a *fatwa* on our northside grammar. He could wax operatic on 'he do' and 'he have', weaving them into long swoops of incredulity. I remember that excuses for not having our exercise done were an art form. Some offenders opted for the epic approach, launching into an account of how 'Me Auntie den called down wit her crowd and sure you couldn't do a tap wit dem in de house,' safe in the knowledge that he'd get browned off with the narrative and roar on to the next fella. Others favoured the understated and creative line: 'De baby et me eck.' Sully's greatest threat was: 'You will all end up as *Echo* boys and messenger boys.' Little did he know that he was threatening us with our dearest wish. *Echo* boys shouted in the street and got paid for it, and messenger boys had bikes!

The lay teachers were all called 'de masters' and the Brothers were 'de monks.' 'De monks' came in all shapes, ages and humours but Lofty was unique. He was the giant who stalked the big boy's yard during Play, his long-limbed prowl as dogged and unswerving as an ice-breaker through a solid pack of boys. I fell foul of Lofty and it was Dave's fault. Among Dave's sermonettes were two particular gems.

'Never answer to a whistle. Dat's very demeaning; only dogs do dat. And never answer to "hey"; remember you have a name.'

One particular day, I was freewheeling around the yard, when a sharp whistle struck my ear. I faltered, remembered Dave's caution, and continued. 'Hey you,' came ringing into the other ear but I pretended not to notice. Suddenly, I found myself nose to navel with Lofty. 'Are you deaf?,' he asked. 'No, Brother,' I answered, 'and I'm not Hey either.' I never even saw the clatter coming.

Reeling away to become invisible in the mob, I made a mental note to be more selective in my acceptance of Dave's proverbs.

Sports were big on the Mon curriculum. A fever seemed to sweep the school when the senior team got into the final of the Harty Cup and the weeks before were fraught with posters and colours and bringing in the money for the small cardboard train ticket. At the crack of dawn on final day we were out of the beds without urging and racing for the railway, our pockets sagging with sandwiches. Before the train roared into daylight beyond the tunnel, we were hoarse. By the time we reached Mallow, we had eaten and drunk our entire store. From there to Limerick we took turns being sick out the windows or standing in the shaky place between two carriages for air. We strode off that train in Limerick, bristling in blue and white and ready for action.

I can remember only the times when we won and the happy havoc as the train rocked homeward to Cork. There was always an impromptu procession from the station up the middle of MacCurtain Street, until the crowd was siphoned off into sidestreets. At last we coasted in the front door, ready to replay the day before the fire.

Religion ran a close second in terms of interest and involvement. Every class was started with a prayer. 'Grace before meals' as one Brother was heard to remark as he watched a timid new teacher stand up before 4B. The prayer was a kind of spiritual sedative; an effort at quelling our restlessness into a semblance of receptivity. Religion class was always before lunch and we listened to the wonderfully horrible deaths of the Christian martyrs to a background of rumbling bellies.

The scamper home at the end of the day was full of shouts and flying caps and tossing the ponytails of sniffy young wans from the convent school. I favoured the horse approach, whipping my imaginary steed past Mullane's shop, giving him his head on Wolfe Tone Street, before we took the corner for home on two hooves in a scatter of gymslips. By the time I hit the Lane I was beginning to flag. The empty house held no attraction. The sack of books was dumped in the caboosh under the stairs and I was off to the Quarry.

The Quarry was an oasis of calm after the energy of the school day. Sometimes I liked to climb the high wall behind the 'new houses,' just to sit and be still. Gradually my eyes would go out of focus and I would float off into a daydream. The sensations I can remember are of the wind tickling the hairs on the backs of my bare legs or the shimmering of green from over the convent wall. Sometimes, I was lulled to the point where I welcomed the impact when I jumped back to earth and trailed my hand for reassurance along the stubby faces of the houses, as I walked down the Lane.

I was also getting lanky and strong and though I knew I'd never match Michael's gift with a hurley, I could hold my own among my own and that was enough. It was in the Mon that the little spark I had for writing was first noted and fanned with praise. Compositions were my joy, and the more difficult the topic the more I relished the challenge. Mr O'Sullivan, our teacher again in fourth class, was quick to oblige.

'Now, boys, for tomorrow, I want four pages on "An

Old Football Boot Tells its Story".'

I hardly heard his warnings about 'wide margins' and 'big writing', my brain was racing with possible approaches. When he brought our corrected copies into the classroom the next morning, I noticed mine was at the top of the heap.

'Christy, stand up. Tell me now boy, what does "melancholy" mean?'

'It means to be sad, sir,' I stuttered.

'Sit down, boy. Now, lads,' he said to the class, 'I want ye to listen to this,' and he began to read my composition. It had taken me ages to write it and I had to defy Dave's command to 'hit the stairs' to get it finished. But I had polished it into a tale of the football boot which had scored the winning goal in the county final, only to be discarded for a new pair by an ungrateful owner.

'And listen to the last line, boys: "I was very melancholy".'

I sat in the scratched desk with throbbing cheeks and the kind of feeling in my chest I often got before crying. 'Never in all my years as a teacher . . . ' he was saying, and I had to distract myself in case I'd disgrace myself. It was a moment of the purest joy. There was something I could do and do well and the future seemed less frightening than before. I remember that feeling vividly to this day because it lasted so briefly.

Neilus had a look on his face that was half fearful, half concerned. It betokened bad news.

'Christy, I think Auntie Nelly is after gettin' hurted. You'd better go down home.'

I was rooted to the schoolyard. All around me, boys

were boiling after ball and playing chasing in the sunlight, their shouts rebounding from the concrete shed. I put my head down on the low wall and started to cry. Neilus called the Brother and I was sent home. Our little house was in agony. The women rocked back and forth on chairs as neighbours fussed around them. I saw Eily Leary filling a kettle from the tap, her tears dripping into the sink. Over the next few awful hours, the story emerged. She had finished tidying up in our house after the dinner and was heading home up Fair Hill, in her black shawl. The small children from the parish schools were surging all around her on the path. At the top of the hill, a parked tractor began to move. ''Twas an act of God it didn't hit a child,' the neighbours said. But it hit Auntie Nelly.

'What kind of God would do a thing like that?' Kay asked angrily, voicing the question we were afraid to ask. No one could answer her. It was the first time I ever saw my father crying. He held himself all the way from work and crumpled just inside the door. We heard his terrible sobs from the front room as the women tried to console him. But there could be no consolation. The little woman with the bright face and clouded eyes had followed Maura and Nan, and left us. And that evening, forgetting I was a 'big boy,' I crept into Pop's lap, burrowing into his broad chest for comfort. I knew then that my childhood was over.